Learning To Be Someone

LEARNING TO BE SOMEONE

A Journey Toward The Light

Elisabeth Anne Parent

Mill City Press

Mill City Press, Inc.
212 3rd Avenue North, Suite 290
Minneapolis, MN 55401
612.455.2294
www.millcitypublishing.com

ISBN-13: 978-1-936780-22-8
LCCN: 2011924800

Cover Design by Melanie Shellito
Typeset by Nate Myers

Printed in the United States of America

TABLE OF CONTENTS

DEDICATION

I want to dedicate my autobiography, first of all to my husband, Richard, who without his constant patience, and support, I wouldn't have been able to fulfill my dream of writing my book. I also want to acknowledge my four sisters and my brother who shared with me the early years of my life which were not without its challenges. Then there's our daughter, Rachelle, who leaves a lasting impact on everyone she meets. There are also three valuable contributors who edited my manuscript and I want to thank Dawna Beausoleil, Margaret Moore, and Dr. Claire Ellis for their expertize and encouragement. Lastly, my Christian friends who were supportive in directing my paths towards God.

INTRODUCTION

It is said that youth is wasted on the young; in my case I had to grow up fast. Along with my siblings, I was a product of parents who lived through the great depression, two wars, and experimented with 'Parenting 101.' In my generation, parents seemed to conform to the TV series, "Father Knows Best", where the parents were the authority and the children knew where they stood in most areas of family dynamics.

Why would I want to share my life story, when I've already lived it? I want to be as transparent and factual about my life experiences as possible by attempting to give a balance view of what I perceived as a child growing up all the way to my adulthood. Also, I have been blessed to have many extraordinary experiences. Hopefully the reader will understand where I came from, what I was going through, and how I got to where I am today, because I know that there are some of you out there that can relate to my story.

How does one go from being a ballroom dancer, to a fashion model, to a beauty queen contestant, then to a New Age follower and teacher of the New Age, and finally a pastor's wife and missionary serving in Africa and Madagascar? Mine was a journey full of uneven roads, and curves, that at times took me away from my true focus, and worthy goals. Instead, I chose well-traveled roads that led me to unpredictable circumstances that created some great adventures, some pain, anguish, and even victories from my Lord. As an author I hope to identify with my readers who might have similar downtrodden paths. Fortunately, at the last turn of the road I finally discovered God's purpose for my life.

"An inebriate is a man who thinks the whole world evolves around him" by O.A. Battista

CHAPTER 1
FIRE OF DEATH

My parents came from different small villages in Quebec, Canada, where large families were prevalent. One could always tell a family's nationality and religion by the size of the family. Being Catholic and French were the only qualifications needed to have a lot of children. Take my mother's parents as an example. They had twenty-one children and among them were five sets of twins.

My parents met just prior to War World II, in a Native mining town called Matachewan, located in Northern Ontario. My father worked as a mill man in the mines, using special tools to chip away the silver and different metals from the large rocks. He also had a part time job as an insurance agent, and after becoming acquainted with my mother at a dance, he hired her as his secretary. And if that didn't keep him busy enough, he played his violin in dance halls every free evening he could find. From a child of five, my father had a strong passion for music, and when given the opportunity to learn the violin, he gladly accepted lessons. Some relative gave him an old violin when he noticed my dad's keen interest in music. So for many years he carried this old violin with him everywhere he went, until he was old enough to play in dance halls and bars. His greatest love of music kept him hopping from one dance hall to another. Along with playing his violin came his social drinking habits, which later became his downfall.

My father was twenty years older than my mother. After my parents' courtship progressed, they married and settled in Matachewan, a town of five hundred people. It has since become a ghost town when the mines closed. At that time many French intermarried with the First Nations people. In fact, my grandmother, on my mom's side, was half Indian from Quebec.

After a few years of marriage my parents were excited when their son James was born, followed by another son, Nelson, and then two daughters named Betty-Anne, (nickname for Elisabeth), and baby Sandra. My dad seemed very proud to have the chance to father children at his older age.

He was very generous with his money, and they were well provided for. They owned a medium-sized home and a large car. By standards back in the forties, they were considered middle class and financially set, but the dark clouds rolled in when dad started coming home quite intoxicated, and arguments began to be the focus of their marriage.

One cold, crisp, clear winter night in February, as the stars sparkled brightly, it appeared evident peace and tranquillity abounded in this small village of Matachewan. No one could have guessed that tragedy would strike from inside our home, when life seemed so calm, and peaceful on the outside. That evening my father was working the graveyard shift at the mine, and the children were tucked in their warm beds fast asleep. Mom settled down comfortably on the couch with her newspaper. As was her habit, she checked on five-month old

Sandra, sleeping soundly in her cradle beside my parents' bed. The roaring fire in the wood stove felt so cozy, in contrast to the freezing temperature outside. After briefly reading Mom felt quite drowsy, and the newspaper fell behind the couch and landed between the plug and the wall socket. In the meanwhile, Mom got up from the couch and went to bed and fell asleep. Homes in those days were not inspected for default wiring, and in a short time the newspaper started to smolder and eventually a fire broke out behind the couch.

In the wee hours of the morning, a framed picture of St. Anthony fell from the bedroom wall on top of mom's head, waking her up abruptly. Screams and cries came from the children's bedrooms, and mom quickly realized that the house was on fire, and that the children were in great danger. James age four, Nelson age three, and Elisabeth, age two, were trapped in that fire. Frantically jumping out of bed, Mom took baby Sandra from the cradle, wrapped her in warm blankets, and put her on the porch floor. Then she crawled back into the house toward my brothers bedroom. Her eyes were now burning, and her vision was blurred with thick clouds of smoke. As she approached their bedroom, it dawned on her that the children were not crying anymore; their little voices seemed silent. An empty eerie feeling came over her, "What if, what if," she whispered over and over. She could not form into words the shocking truth, but instead pushed the fatal thought out of her mind. When she finally got to the boys' room, James and Nelson were lying still on the floor. Panic stricken, Mom dragged them carefully out to the porch, hoping for a miracle. A silent scream gripped her throat as she attempted to make a final rescue to save Betty-Anne. Now all three small bodies lay lifeless on the floor, beside the squirming baby, Sandra. As the fire trucks drove up to the burning house, people began running toward the blazing fire fearing the worst.

When Dad was contacted at work and told to come home quickly, his house was on fire, he began to panic. He finally arrived home, and frantically looked for Mom and the children. There was a lot of confusion, with people running around trying to help wherever they could. As Dad walked around in shock, he kept repeating to anyone who approached him, "I don't care about losing my house, as long as my family is safe and alive."

Finally he was directed to a neighbor's home where Mom and the children were staying. Upon entering the living room he noticed despair on Mom's face, and knew that tragedy had struck. The doctor was stooping over the three children trying to revive them, but to no avail. They had died of smoke inhalation during the fire, and nothing short of a miracle could save them. No miracle was seen that night, except for one small 6 month old baby, Sandra, who was spared, and the doctor gave her a clear bill of health.

I suppose the best way to describe the feelings that occur after an enormous loss like this, is to liken it to an ice storm, when freezing rain beats down on the gentle slender branches, time after time. Then the temperature gradually drops until they begin to bend downward further from the heavy ice . It seems from the extra weight on the branches, they are ready to snap, and break off completely from the heavily laden tree. But when you examine it closer, a small ray of sunlight breaks through, and ever so gently the sun begins to melt the heavily iced twigs, until they spring back to their original shape and position. Loss is never forever, even though the scars of deep tragedy remain.

Baby Sandra became Mom's reason to go on living, during the stormy dark days ahead. She also gave Mom hope that their fragmented lives could gradually mend and heal.

The funeral took place in the only large Catholic church on a hill overlooking the river and town. Inside the church, up front, stood three small precious caskets standing neatly in a row. In place of the children's laughter, was replaced by a dead silence that permeated within the church. There in the front pews sat Mom and Dad, and few close friends huddled beside them. Tears of remorse were falling rapidly down our parents cheeks, as they faced the sharp painful reality of never seeing their children again on this earth. As the priest raised his voice to speak, the echo of emptiness left his voice barely audible. What made matters worse was that none of my parents' family could attend the funeral, due to the cold snowy winter that made the long-distance trip impossible.

The Bible makes it clear that there is life after death. There is a temporal rest in the grave, and an assurance that when Christ returns He will bring His rewards with him. This same Book speaks about our eternal dwelling with Christ in the Book of Revelation 21: 3, 4 NIV.

"Now the dwelling of God is with men, and he will live with them...He will wipe every tear from their eyes. There will be no more death or mourning or crying or pain, for the old order of things has passed away."

Not long after my brothers and sister were buried, Mom felt sick and visited the doctor. He confirmed what she thought to be true, that she was pregnant once more. She was going to have another child, her fifth baby, Elisabeth. However, the doctor cautioned her that due to her frail body, and deep losses, she might not be able to carry this baby throughout the nine months.

I know when my parents gazed lovingly into my crib, the thoughts of "God, how are we going to disrupt her life?"were never there. It just happened. So much has been written of the great history of England's Queen Elisabeth I and II. But nothing has ever been told about my sister Elisabeth I who died so tragically and so very young. I became known as Elisabeth II. Was I a replacement, one name fits all, or does grief dictate it to be so?

Life being full of unexpected surprises, I was born a healthy strong baby, weighing more than all the other children at birth. Then fifteen months later another baby girl, Nadine, arrived eager to live life to the fullest. Despite the fact that my parents had three healthy, lively daughters, my dad grew more and more sullen and depressed. He would spend more time at the hotel drinking with his buddies hoping to bury his pain and the loss of his three small children. Frequently he would come home late missing supper. Staggering into the house, he would start cursing Mom, and blaming her for the children's deaths. These were hard times for both my parents as they tried to struggle alone with their grief without any marriage counseling.

One day Dad was babysitting us three girls while Mom was visiting a neighbor. Dad enjoyed playing with us when he had time, and we enjoyed being with him on these occasions. Dad decided to dress us up in our pretty frilly silk dresses that Mom had made. The dresses were the same color, so we looked like triplets. When Mom came back home she found Dad and us gone, and began to panic. Ever since the fire Mom had became overprotective of us, and would rarely let us out of her sight. She knew that Dad must have taken us somewhere, and she had a hunch she knew where to find us. Rounding the corner and going toward the stores, she spotted us through the hotel window. There we were sitting tall on the bar stools, with our short legs dangling, drinking milk while Dad drank his glass of liquor. Mom marched promptly into the hotel and without saying a word to Dad, took us down off the stools. We were led out the door toward home.

Not long after that episode, Mom pleaded with Dad to move away from Matachewan, this small mining town with several hotels, held no future for her children to obtain proper schooling, and a fulfilled life. At first my Dad took Mom seriously and began to pack his belongings in boxes. He even told the neighbors that we were moving soon. Then one night, a week before our scheduled move to a larger community called Haileybury, Dad met up with his drinking buddies, and when he returned home late one night, he staggered unto the porch. Mom took one look at him and knew that he had changed his mind about starting life over in a different city.

Mom tried to reason with him when he was sober the next day about moving away to Haileybury. She felt so bewildered, and alone with this problem. She just knew she couldn't continue living in Matachewan, with its hurtful memories. After much thought and pleading Mom told him that she planned to visit her parents' home, and was taking the three small girls with her. Mom's parents had recently moved from Quebec to Hamilton in Southern Ontario, far away from where we lived. As Mom finished packing the last suitcase, Dad realized that we would never return to live with him again. I imagine we hugged Dad, and wondered why he wasn't coming with us. Years later when looking back at the scene, I could only imagine how difficult it was for him to say goodbye to his daughters. When all the suitcases were packed and we said our goodbyes we climbed into the taxi cab that drove us several hundred miles south to Hamilton. I wasn't born yet to remember how devastating the fire and its losses had on my parents. However, years later when I was about eight years old, I felt abandoned by my father.

As a child I used to wonder if Mom wanted any more children after losing her three oldest ones in a house fire. As an adult with a child of my own I finally gathered up the courage to ask her and, she reassured me that she was very happy that more children were added to her home.

It was evident that Mom felt these losses all her life, especially when these children's birthdays would come up. Her dark moods and depressions would set in, and it seemed obvious that my parent's losses had caused their marriage to end. This loss began a new jouney in all our lives.

"The only permanence in life is change", by Vonnegut

CHAPTER 2

ADJUSTING TO NEW SURROUNDINGS

Life at my grandparents' home where most of their older children lived, became quite exciting for us. For the first time we met a lot of aunts and uncles and a slew of cousins who fussed over us. We enjoyed their constant attention sharing activities with our new-found cousins.

The large city of Hamilton known for its steel industry, seemed so large and gigantic to us. We were forever looking up at the tall buildings when we went shopping or strolling in the park. Sunday was a fun day for our large extended family.

During the summer when we would come home after church, a huge picnic lunch was packed, as we headed for the beautiful park near the mountain brow. There we would spread blankets and cushions on the ground, and enjoy sandwiches, cookies and refreshments. It seemed our Sunday picnics attracted one particular intruder, a red well-fed squirrel. In my excitement, I screamed with glee, "our pet red squirrel came to visit with us, let's feed him some peanuts." Mom took the bag of peanuts she carried with her just in case. He would boldly jump onto our blanket hoping for a tidbit. "Here is your favourite food, friend." He didn't wait for an invitation as he took the shell peanuts from my hands. "Do you know red squirrel I have to find you a nickname so that everytime we see you in the park you will come to us for your favourite food."

Eventually I nicknamed him 'Red Flash' because of his colour, and his quick movements. He became my favorite pet, and so delightful to have around. I'd never met such a tame, friendly squirrel quite like him. After we finished eating, and ready for our walk through the park I'd say to 'Flash', "See you next Sunday and we can have another picnic together." Unfortunately, when we came the next Sunday to the park to have our picnic Red Flash was nowhere to be seen, and I felt a little sad that he never came back to greet us ever again at the park.

The grown ups would be talking in French while we children stayed in front of them, skipping and jumping about. At one point, Sandy said, " see who can jump the highest". Since we all had a competitive spirit, we would do our best to see who could jump the highest.

During the late afternoon Mom would treat us to a six cent ice cream cone. There were only three flavors back then, chocolate, french vanilla, and strawberry. I would frequently choose french vanilla. Today, I fear there are too many flavors that I like. Then we would find a spot in the park to sit and rest. On many occasions, we listened to the outdoor orchestra playing the modern tunes of Glen Miller and Lawrence Welk. Crowds would gather around the bandstand tapping their toes to the music, and singing the catchy tunes. Looks of jubilance and contentment were written on many faces. The future was bright and promising for everyone now that World War II had ended.

My grandparents' house was like a hotel most of the time, full of people traffic. There's a nursery rhyme that goes like this: "There was an old woman who lived in a shoe; she had so many children she didn't know what to do." Life was quite hectic, yet it carried an atmosphere of fun and laughter for a large family of aunts, uncles and cousins all living in my grandparents nineteen-room house. Some of my uncles who had fought in World War II came back with changed attitudes from their time spent on the front lines in Holland and Italy. They didn't share any of their own experiences, except for a few general stories. One time one of my cousins asked uncle John what it was like in Amsterdam, Holland fighting against German soldiers? "Well, he said I recall a time when my best friends were in a boat in the Amsterdam Canal fighting against the enemy Germans. It was a difficult and hard fight because a bullet went right through my arm and killed my best friend fighting beside me." "Those were hard times he said and the losses were great on both sides." I guess there was some perks though, because I discovered a picture of me in an old war book from Holland sitting on an old tank waving and yelling out, 'victory is ours. And my name was written down below as a Canadian soldier who helped rescue Holland from the enemies."

Years later when I visited a relative in Holland I did discover an old war time book with the same picture my uncle described to us years later.

Unfortunately, during their time overseas, they picked up habits of drinking and smoking. The war had a big effect on many families, but we were grateful that there had been no casualties in our family.

Since finances were very tight, now that my mother was separated from Dad , she tried to make a living for herself and her girls. However, she was a frail person and would fall sick easily. She gradually found a job working at the Westinghouse plant, but found the work very hard and tedious. Lifting heavy boxes and equipment back and forth to different store rooms, caused a lot of pain to her back. Mom would come home from work to say, "lifting heavy boxes all day isn't what I call an easy job, and I don't know how long I can take this."She found the work so strenuous she had to quit. In the meantime, she found another job that didn't pay as much, but it was easier work.

My sisters and I were now enrolled in a Catholic elementary school not far from our grandparents' house, so we were able to walk home from school everyday. We enjoyed school, especially recess where we played hopscotch and skipped the rope with other children.

We were afraid of some of the nuns who taught us because they were very strict. The strap was used often and I seemed to be the recipient of many straps. If I was a few minutes late for school or didn't read a story from the reader fast enough in front of the class, some whacks on my bare hands told me that my teacher did not care about me enough to find out what my problem was. Other times the nun would say, "Betty-Anne you will have to learn to write with your right hand instead of your left, because it is a right handed world, and in order for you to fit in you must change." I guess there was enough Irish stubbornness for me to keep writing with my left hand, despite the consequences.

How well I remember my grandparents' huge comfortable home that faced the mountain brow and overlooked another city below. In the summer evenings, part of the family would cross the street and sit on the edge of a short stone wall. Gazing upon the shining, dancing stars above, one could see the harbor bay smack in the middle of the city with many large boats. It was a sight to behold all the lights from the city and the ships in the bay. Other nights we would be found sitting in rocking chairs on the porch. My grandfather was proud that he had made benches, and huge rocking chairs from oak trees to furnish the porch. I grew to love this city more than I realized. I never got tired of traveling on the buses with my mom down to the city below. What is so unique about Hamilton is that a city stands on top of another city, and when you descend the mountain, either by car or bus, the roads are windy and steep. On occasion, rocks from the side of the mountains have come tumbling down crashing on the road below, just barely missing oncoming cars.

I never forgot the time my cousin Gilbert with his sisters Judy and Linda and I, were looking below at the mountain brow to see how steep it was. At that moment Gilbert tried to persuade us to grab a branch near by and to swing all the way down the mountain like Tarzan and Jane. We were afraid to grab the branch, and Gilbert began calling us 'scaredy cats' why don't you and Judy show me how brave you can be and act like Tarzan, it's as easy as drinking lemonade, so on the count of three grab the long branch and swing." When he realized that we were not going to challenge him and act like Tarzans, he decided he would show us his brave side so he grabbed the branch with two hands. As he began to swing fast and hard, the branch broke and he fell down the mountain. Instantly, we ran home for help. Poor Gilbert was badly injured and it took some time before he fully recuperated. But we never heard another word from Gilbert about swinging from a branch like Tarzan and Jane again.

"Danger feared is folly; danger faced is freedom" by Raymond Edman

CHAPTER 3

DANGEROUS INTRUDER

One warm summer night, near the mountain brow where we lived, a tragedy almost took my mother's life. A few months before our old fashioned radio had a special broadcast announcing that a violent killer had escaped from the Hamilton prison and was loose in our area. Folks were warned not to go out on the streets after dark. People were in fear and bondage in their homes. Each day my relatives would sit around the radio, eagerly hoping for the good news that the killer had been caught and locked away. The police were working day and night trying to find the killer, but he was crafty and too fast for them. The stress was taking its toll. My relatives would go to bed with kitchen knives, and glass bottles of all shapes and colors. It seemed like we'd been hostages for an eternity. This particular night, when we were all asleep, my mother heard a crashing sound on the balcony next to her room. She tried to scream but no sound came out. She froze, knowing that there was someone out there wanting to come in. She was certain she saw someone trying to pry the balcony door open. Mom immediately awakened her sister. Her heart was pounding so rapidly she thought she would have a heart attack. She gave her an urgent shove, finally waking her up, and told her what was happening. Just then a tall slender man entered the room and came creeping towards the bed. My aunt screamed so loudly that she woke the entire household. Just as the man plunged towards her to cover her mouth, my uncles ran into the room with bottles in their hands, poised, ready to hit the guy. The man ran back to the one storey balcony and took a flying leap to the ground.

By then, everyone was wide awake and clinging to each other, eager to hear what was going on. My uncle called the police station right away to report what had happened. The police arrived at our house later and searched the yard, front and back. There, beside the dog house lay my uncle's dog. It had been killed. That's why he hadn't barked when the intruder broke into our house. Inside the dog house was a man with his arms tightly hugging his legs and shaking. When they brought him to the police station, they identified him as the man who had escaped from the Hamilton prison months before. Everybody in the household gave a sigh of relief when the violent killer was put back in prison to await his trail. The court pronounced him guilty of murder on a few counts and he remained locked away. The excitement and fear finally faded. No more kitchen knives or glass bottles were found beside the beds at night. Life finally settled down to a normal pace for everyone.

No sooner did one near tragedy pass than another occurred. My grandmother had been bed ridden with cancer for a long time. My two sisters and I took turns sharing afternoon naps with her. The novelty of napping with my grandmother almost every day wore off quickly as I was bored and restless. One spring day, Grandmother was taken to the hospital for good, never to return home to us. I remember her parting words to us, "Children don't forget to be good girls for your mother by listening when she asks you to do something. When you finish eating help her by carrying your dishes to the sink and wash and dry them. Also, it's very important to thank her for being so good to you and being your special mother." Then one after the other, we gave our little speeches to Grandmother. Before she left, my sister Nadine said, "Grandmother, why don't you put on your slippers and come downstairs to eat? We can have something to eat together and you will feel all better, you'll see". This chapter of Grandmother's life was over, but our memories of her olive skin, dark brown eyes and her hair net on her head, live vividly in her grandchildren's minds.

Grandmother left a legacy of knowledge and experiences behind. Not only did she give birth to over eighteen children, including a few sets of twins, she was very knowledgeable with identifying various types of herbs for medicinal purposes. She was known as a herbalist in her community. Many times she would send my mom to find different types of herbs in the fields to make health potions for her sick neighbors.

"Look for the good, not the evil, in the conduct of members of the family" by Leo Rosten

CHAPTER 4

THE EXTENDED FAMILY

A few years later, after Mom's divorce from Dad, she re-married, and a new step-father became part of our lives. Gradually our family grew from three to six children; five girls and one boy. Life became very busy for my parents, as the children were full of energy and mischief. However, it became a real challenge to Mom as her workload increased, because washing and ironing took such a long time, not like today with modern appliances.

Living in an extended family environment made life hectic and unstable, but as children, we were resilient and preoccupied ourselves with games and fun, rather then fretting about adult problems. Unknown to us, Mom was running away from her tragedy and marriage in Northern Ontario, where her three children were buried. Her unresolved grief and guilt caused her to jump into another unstable relationship that brought a lot of hardship and pain for all of us. Arguments were frequent between our parents, and gradually the children felt insecure and timid when speaking to adults. Despite the conflicts though, we children were able to keep close to one another in later years. We knew our parents loved us even though they didn't know how to show it consistently.

One time, my sister Susan, who was about two years old, full of energy, and quick of mind, decided to play a trick on Mom by hiding. One of Susan's favorite games was hide-and-seek, and she proceeded to hide herself in an undesirable place. Just before lunch time Mom searched for Susan everywhere in the house, and she even went outside calling her name, but Susan didn't answer. Finally Mom went back into the house, and decided to start lunch hoping that Susan would be hungry enough to come out of her hiding place. It wasn't until Mom opened the oven door that she found Susan, snuggled up in the back of the oven not wanting to get caught. Mom shuddered to think what could have happened if she had put on oven before she put the food in.

One day after school Mom asked, "Betty Anne would you dress Denise, my youngest sister, in her burgundy dress and take her for a ride in her carriage. Here is a list of groceries to buy at the store. Lifting her into big carriage, I proudly pushed it down the street, pretending Denise was my child. I tried to be careful not to tip the carriage when we mounted the high curb, but the carriage slipped off the edge and Denise came tumbling over the side and fell onto the muddy street. Her pretty dress was full of mud, not to mention her face and arms. Fortunately, the only thing that was hurt was her pride. We both walked to the store ever so slowly with her both hands firmly on the bar of the carriage while pushing the carriage carefully down the street. It was obvious she'd made up her mind that she wasn't going to get back into that carriage again.

As a child Denise had a passion for animals and insects of all assortments. Since Mom had a passion for photography, there are several photos of Denise feeding some animal whether it was a dog or cat, insects or mice. There is one photo in particular of Denise at two years old, sitting on the backyard tire swing feeding a mouse with cheese. Not to mention, back in house there were plenty of grasshoppers, bees, and other insects living in jars of all shapes and sizes.

On one rare occasion our parents brought us to a local restaurant for a meal. When the waitress asked us what we would like to order Denise piped up and said, "I would like a hot dog for my grasshoppers please, and pointed to them in her jar." The waitress looked a bit surprised, but she went along with Denise's request and said, "One hot dog coming up for the starving grasshoppers." Needless to say, Denise fed her grasshoppers a piece of her own hot dog. If I'm not mistaken she might have had names picked out for them.

A picture of my brother Gregory with curly long blonde hair still stands out in my mind. At a very young age of two he would climb up on the kitchen counter, pick up the heavy black telephone, and say in his not very clear English, "allô, allô". Of course there was no one on the other line, but he loved to talk on the telephone just the same. It paid off because later on in his career he was always dealing with telephones and customers.

"Nostalgia is a release from reality, far safer than drugs and alcohol" Social Studies

CHAPTER 5
FOND MEMORIES

Some of these historical facts about life in the 50's were taken from the internet, and information about Crystal Beach, Ontario, Canada, was taken from a 2001 Crystal Beach historical calendar published by Cathy Herbert Ridgeway, Ontario Canada.

What was it like living in the 1950's and 1960's?

Well, for one thing there were several reports on the1950's Contaminated Polio Vaccines -- a Deadly Cure. The government had initiated the mandatory polio vaccination programs in 1955. Prior to this, polio had killed or crippled thousands of children and adults worldwide. Attacking the central nervous system, this viral infection was transmitted by human contact, sewage and even by contaminated milk. Victims who contracted polio would incubate the virus in their intestines, where it would multiply before entering the lymphatic system. Eventually the virus would penetrate the nerves and travel along nerve paths, destroying neurons and rendering the muscles connected to them paralyzed.

In fact, in the mid 50's my brother Gregory came down with a deadly virus and he was very ill with high fever and a stomach ache. I remember one day when he said to mother in a weak voice and tears in his eyes, "Am I going to die mom?" It seemed mother gave him the answer he needed to hear because he shortly fell asleep with a serene expression on his face. My mother thought Gregory might have contacted polio through this polio epidemic going around, because he couldn't move his legs for a few days. Fortunately, it wasn't polio but the Asiatic flu that struck young children especially. Unfortunately, several children died of this deadly virus that summer.

What about prime time TV ? As a child I remember watching all the western movies like Long Ranger and Zorro, who always rescued the victim from the villain., then there was Roy Rogers and Dale Evans, and many others. Of course those were the days without TV remote controls. Everybody had to get off the couch to turn the channel. What a hardship_

I will never forget the popular music we danced to in the 50's such as the jive, and the twist. We adored dancing to Elvis Presley's music, and second in line were the Beatles. As teens we used to dress up like them and try to imitate their singing style.

Ballroom dancing was a big hit, too, in the 1950's and 60's. Since my mom was a ballroom dancing teacher her children learned how to do the various steps.

The 50's was a time of peace and a safe atmosphere for children. Youngsters were free to roam around the neighborhood without worry of being abducted. Parents knew that if their children did something wrong, they could trust other adults to correct them and set them straight. The philosophy 'that it takes an entire community to raise children' was taken seriously, and put into action. Family and Children's Aid didn't take an active role in those day, but in some family incidents it would have been helpful.

Parents were responsible for disciplining and raising their children with firmness and respect. And I believe that this was all part of parental love. Thus, there were fewer delinquent teenagers on drugs or alcohol than we see today. Back then TV and the media didn't have a big influence on children. Violent and sexual movies were prohibited and not available for TV viewing. Children were more creative in making up their own games and solving some of their own problems. The 50's was one of the greatest and most peaceful eras for raising children. Trust and honesty were paramount. We tried to live the honest life as children, but when something else caught our fancy, we fell short. Only after parents set children straight, did they get back on track.

One summer my mom bought my brother Gregory a medium-sized tent for his birthday. Of course we were all excited about this because we had other plans in the making. We told mom we'd be playing cards in the tent until it was time to eat lunch. However, that wasn't entirely true. One unusual hot humid day, all six of us went into the tent to play card games. Since it was our brother's tent, he made up some rules on how to play black jacks, and some of the losers ended up taking off their socks, sandals, and shirts. The only remaining clothes we kept on were our undershirts and shorts.

One particular day, while in the tent playing black jacks, out of boredom, one of us suggested, "why don't we all go down to the train station to see if there were any beggars sleeping on the trains, and we all agreed out of boredom to explore the beggars on the train." Off we went fully dressed, creeping as quietly as possible away from the tent until we were out of sight from home. When we arrived at the train track we noticed the trains were slowly pulling out from the train station. Quickly a few of us children shouted, "jump unto the train and stay down." Once inside one of the carts we were searching for beggars that we had heard might be found there. Frightened we carefully stepped into some hay when a beggar suddenly jumped up from the hay with an empty bottle of whiskey. He frightened us so much that all we screamed at the top of our lungs and jumped off slow-moving train all excited and sweaty.

From there we noticed a broken telephone pole that was lying beside the road. One of my siblings had a light bulb experience excitingly said, " Why don't we drag the post to the small hill across the street and make a long teeter totter." It was difficult to drag and heavy to lift and in the process we accumulated a lot of slivers in our hands, but did we care, not one bit.

The awkward part was trying to stay on one end of the teeter totter without slipping down and falling unto the ground. It must have been Sandra the oldest who said, "alright this is the rule, three of us are to sit on one end of the pole while three others sit on the other end." At first it sounded okay until three of us would be held up in the air for a long period of time causing more slivers on our knees and hands, while the other three stayed put on the ground at the other end laughing their heads off.. After awhile we all had enough of being suspended in the air with slivers and were eager to head home.

When we arrived home for lunch, we sneaked back into the tent awaiting mom's call to eat.

What about the fashions that teenage girls liked to wear? The pleated short skirts called skorts were really in style. I saved up enough money from my babysitting job to buy a pale blue pleated short skirt, and buckskin, off-white shoes that were so cool, so I thought! Of course, both sexes wore saddle shoes and white socks. They were a real hit. The guys slicked their hair with greasy cream like Brylcream to keep it in place.

Guys wore short leather jackets and shirts with collars worn straight up. Nice modest dresses were in vogue too, along with classy fashion trends.

In the 1950's, our family lived across the street from Queen Circle park where we played touch tag and British football. There were a few large war monuments with inscriptions written of heroic soldiers from World War II. One day my sister Nadine climbed on top of one of the war monuments, and in jest, and not thinking of the consequences, I pulled her off. Unfortunately, she fell and fractured her collar bone. My face went ashen as I realized what I did. Frightened and scared I cried out, "Are you alright?" "I am so sorry for hurting you." "When you feel better you can do the same to me then we will be even." Mom heard the commotion and the excitment in our voices, and she quickly came out of the house, and eagerly asked, "Why is Nadine lying on the ground?" I slowly replied, "well she sort of fell and I kind of pulled her from the monument to the ground." "It was an accident and I am sorry." Needless to say, all of us were banned from the Queen Circle for a few weeks.

I suppose if anyone would ask me today, what was my favorite place I lived as a child, , I wouldn't hesitate to say Crystal Beach. Crystal Beach is near Fort Erie, on the Canadian side and Buffalo, New York on the U.S. side. Crystal Beach Amusement Park was famous for its vivid green grass and flower beds. In an advertisement from 1943, the Park boasted: "Gorgeous Horticulture Gardens with bordered paths".

Throughout its history, Crystal Beach Park had a great variety of memorable attractions. Some rides came and went. There were several rides we would try every summer. The Octopus, which swirled its cars at the end of long arms was one. The Old Mill, or Tunnel of Love, was always a favorite During the forty-one years that Crystal Beach Amusement

Park was in operation, from 1948 to 1989, the Comet Roller Coaster was the greatest attraction. It was also one of my preferred rides, and one of great risk. My sisters and I would take turns standing with our arms waving in the air as we went down the longest and fastest track. Next to the largest roller coaster ride in New York, Crystal Beach's was the second largest. The Cyclone Roller Coaster was one of three built in 1927 by Harry Traver, and the only one in Canada at that time. A nurse was on duty at all times to care for the riders who succumbed to this perilous adventure. As much fun as it was to ride the coaster, there was a downside as well.

A tragedy that took a life is something we will never forget. Part of the coaster was built on the land and the other part was built in the waters of Lake Erie. One hot summer day, as I was walking toward the roller coast, I heard a woman screaming from the Cyclone Roller Coaster. She was yelling and screaming and I knew there must have been a tragedy. A woman was coming off the ride yelling frantically that her baby had fallen out of her arms while they rode the roller coaster. The woman held her baby in her arms while riding on the high roller coaster, when suddenly the baby slipped from her arms and landed on the ground below. The doctor and nurse were at the scene checking the baby carefully for vital signs, but it was too late. What a sad event that was. The ride was shut down for the remaining week to commemorate the sad event. Stricter rules were enforced, and parents were not permitted to bring their child under five years old on the roller coaster.

There were a few semi-favorite rides I enjoyed like the Looper. There were ten cars which accommodated two riders apiece, followed around a circular track, the looping motion of each controlled individually by a foot pedal. The feature of self-operation was a special characteristic of this popular amusement. Each rider, using his own pedal, tried to keep the other upside-down as the car followed around the track. It was a competition to control this topsy-turvy situation. One was almost certain to lose any pocket change.

My least preferred ride was the "Rotary". And I'll explain why. This was truly the most embarrassing event I've ever had to suffer through. When you enter the rotary, which is a long circular wall, which at first moves slowly around and around then it speeds up and your body is sucked to the wall which spins faster and faster then the floor separates from the rotary as it descends several feet down. That was scary enough, but to make matters worse my stomach was spinning as well, and I could feel my food coming up and I felt like I wanted to vomit, at the same time my eyes began to be one big blur. Guess what happened next? Suddenly I cried out to warn eveyone, " I am going to be sick and I need to get off right now." It was too late the vomit flew out of my mouth and hit the disgusted faces around me, and like me they couldn't escape. When the rotary finally stopped, I was the first one to run from the ride without looking back at their dripping, angry faces.

Who could ever forget the startling air jets and the "hissing"sound, on a walk through the Magic Carpet? One encountered crazy mirrors, dark alleyways, wooden slides, falling walls and crooked floors all in this walk-through. It was a challenge to step on the lily pads, without losing one's balance and ending up with a wet foot. Opening for the 1947 season, the ride finished with a trip down the "magic carpet", a mechanically driven belt moving over steel rollers. Because of liability concerns it closed in 1972. The ride was then renamed The Magic Palace, as it resembled an Arabian palace, with its imposing turrets.

Fast foods back then consisted of home made french fries, hamburgers, onion rings, popcorn, swallowed down with glass bottled soft drinks. However, what would a visit to the Crystal

Beach Park be without one of Hall's famous suckers? Among the regular flavors were cinnamon, lemon, butterscotch, peanut and coconut. The large metal drums that held the suckers were almost always swarming with bees.

The rock garden at Crystal Beach was a hillside virtually ablaze with color. One would pass by it en route to catch the ***Canadiana*** back to Buffalo. The ***Canadiana*** was probably the most loved ship to ply the waters between Crystal Beach and Buffalo. In operation from 1910 to 1956, it was estimated that she carried 18,400,000 passengers. She made six round trips daily, for a total of one hundred and forty-four miles a day.

Why is the Beach called "Crystal Beach"? Of course, everyone who has ever swum there knows that when the sun glistens on the sand , crystal-like particles of sand shimmer brightly. As a child of ten I recall when people in the Comet Roller Coaster would scream and yell as they would go up and down the ride, and how coins fell out of their pockets and land smack into Crystal Beach. At that moment, wechildren would dive into the water and swim down to the bottom of the lake and attempt to rescue the lost coins. Of course, we knew just what we would spend the money on. We'd run from one ride to another until the money ran out.

Among the many photographs taken of the world-famous Crystal Ballroom, one picture evokes memories of a special time in its life. With the sliding glass door opened, visitors could walk freely in and out of the building, or sit on promenade benches to admire the immense maple floor; waxed and polished to a mirror-like finish. Dancers were only a step away from enjoying the cool night breezes off Lake Erie. The 1925 architecture and decor were ahead of their time, with the levered construction creating an unobstructed dance floor. Many of the well-known orchestras performed here, including Glenn

Miller, the Dorsey Brothers, Les Brown, Woody Herman, and Artie Shaw.

The popular song, "On the Move Again" seemed like it was composed especially for our family. This time the move was to the countryside near the city of Oakville. Six children, two adults, one dog and one cat with a litter of kittens, piled into the old Dodge station wagon. We were happy to start another adventurous move. My stepfather found a job near Oakville which gave him more responsibility as a manager of a company. We arrived at our country home all eager to explore that massive place. The white house had large windows trimmed with black shutters. My favorite window was the contour bay in the living room.

As I looked out, I could see the open fields and huge trees in a distance. The driveway was very long and wide with large even rows of evergreen trees. The house stood on 200 acres of land with a huge gray barn some distance behind the house. It was the most beautiful house we had ever seen. Inside the house was an immense kitchen with swinging French doors and a big pantry, a large hallway and three sizeable bedrooms. The living room was my favorite. In the middle stood a gray brick fireplace which took up one side of the wall. To the left of the fireplace was my beautiful bay contour window with its striking view of the countryside. The upstairs had a separate apartment that my stepfather eventually rented out to a Dutch family with two sets of twins. This couple from Holland had an unusual story to tell. They met in Canada at a Roman Catholic Church. His wife was a nun and he was a priest. They met, fell in love, left their positions in the church, and the rest is history.

After the large moving truck arrived at our new home, the children took turns carrying boxes of clothes inside. When we had carried all we could, we decided we needed time out, and immediately ran to the barn to explore. How happy we were to find a few piles of hay. We didn't waste any time climbing the high beams in order to plunge into the hay lofts.

The country setting seemed so peaceful and tranquil that it soon made a difference in our family. Since we'd moved to Oakville after school was finished, we had the summer to explore our new surroundings. There were apple and pear trees around one side of the house whose fruit we could hardly wait to pick. When some of the fruit finally fell to the ground and rotted, my sisters and brother would have delightful games throwing fruits at each other.

On the next farm we noticed a young man in his late teens driving a large tractor that pulled a roller tiller. We were fascinated by the tiller which dug deep into the ground, tearing up the dirt and leaving long even rows. As we watched the young man working, we all wished for our first ride on a tractor. But Mom had warned us never to ride on one for fear of someone getting hurt.

One hot summer day, as we were standing near the fence wishing we could ride on the tractor, the young man stopped the tractor right in front of us and in a friendly voice, introduced himself. He had a British accent and a charming smile. He introduced himself as David, and told us that he had come from Britain a year ago and was eighteen years old. He wanted to know our names particularly mysisters Nadine and Sandra. Nadine spoke up first and boldly told him our names. I was too bashful to say anything to him. "Would you all like a ride on the tractor?" asked David. "Would we!" We all eagerly moved our heads up and down in the affirmative, despite the warning from our mom.

All six of us eagerly climbed aboard looking a little frightened and guilty. Each of us grabbed onto something to keep our balance. David started up the tractor and slowly crawled around the field with the disk trailing behind, cutting the dirt, and leaving symmetrical even rows. This was a lot of fun, and we didn't mind the rough ride. At one point I became quite dizzy from going around and around. Suddenly I looked down on the ground, and felt more dizzy in my head and stomach. Before I knew it, I had slipped off the tractor and was pinned under the left tractor wheel, the heavy disk not far behind me. I had long hair and I felt the end of my hair being pulled under the tiller. Finally, my oldest sister Sandra notice me missing, and started to scream for David to stop. If it wasn't for Sandra who saved my life, I would not be alive today to write my life story.

Immediately everybody jumped off to see where I'd landed. David was able to pull my left leg from under the wheel and it felt quite sore and throbbed. I managed to hobble home with Sandra and Nadine holding onto me. I knew if I told my mom and stepfather what had happened it would ruin our chances of going to the all-night drive-in theater where we planned to go that Friday evening. Back in the 50's and 60's, the main entertainment for families was going to the drive-in theater. This tradition involved children changing into pyjamas before leaving the house, and carrying some blankets to the car, because the movies finished in the wee hours of the morning. Before I could change into my pyjamas though, my sister had the bright idea to wrap my leg tightly with an elastic bandage before leaving the house.

When we arrived at our destination, my leg was throbbing, because the bandage was cutting off the circulation in my leg. I made an excuse to my mom that I needed to use the washroom. Once inside I quickly tore off the elastic bandage and finally found relief as the numbness subsided. Upon returning to the car I was able to enjoy the family movies projected on an immense screen. The best part about this injury was that we kept this secret from our parents for many years to come.

The 1950's could very well be the end of the innocent age.

"When you're through changing you're through" by Bruce Barton

CHAPTER 6

ONCE A CATHOLIC ALWAYS A CATHOLIC

"Once a Catholic always a Catholic"-- these words echoed down the hallway of my youth. They were spoken by a Catholic priest where my family attended church every Sunday morning. We were raised devoted Catholics. My mother would take us to church every Sunday where we sat silently in the pews, and listened to the priest perform Mass in Latin. The Catholic Church that we went to most of the time, stood on a large hill overlooking the city. The gothic structure and vastness of the building created a sense of reverence. My life in the Catholic church finally came to an end in my early twenties, despite my mother's plea that I remain in this traditional church.

The next school year started and all of us children along with our dog, walked to the end of our incredibly long driveway. There we waited for the big yellow school bus that picked us up. We had mixed feelings about starting a brand new school again, but we did anticipate making friends. Since the Catholic school was out of our area, my sister Sandra and I had to go to a public elementary school. We had never attended a public school before, and we wondered if we would stick out like sore thumbs. In those days, Catholic and Protestant schools were at odds. I recall attending one Catholic school, and a Protestant school stood right beside it. There was a lot of name calling, and physical fights among the students on both sides of the fence.

The first week of school was a little tense for my oldest sister, Sandra and me, because we knew no one, and felt somewhat shy and awkward. Our grade eight teacher was also the principal of the school, and was very strict. We were on our best behavior trying to please our teacher because he was anti-Catholic, and extremely strict. My sister and I would offer to clean the blackboards and carry books for him. However, try as we did, we were never accepted by the teacher or many of the students. They would make fun of our Catholic religion and our lack of Bible knowledge. The teacher would make my sister or me read certain Bible passages in front of the class. Knowing that we were not familiar with the Bible, he would start laughing out loud. Some of the students would join the teacher in this unfair game. We knew we didn't stand a chance against them. We also knew that our family was poor and carried no voice to correct this injustice, so we suffered in silence.

At times we would see the principal go into his office to strap a young girl or boy who was misbehaving. His booming voice could be heard as he said to the youngster, "Do you know why you are here to be punished?" And of course the little boy or girl would start sobbing and would say, between sobs, "I don't know why. Please don't hurt me." Then the principal would ignore the sobs, and strap the little hands as hard as he could several times. Migraine headaches and upset stomachs began to be an occasional part of my school life.

One day, in mid-May at dismissal, our teacher marched up to my sister and I, and told us not to bother coming back. We were not wanted here. We were deeply concerned, because it was only another month until graduation. We tried to reason with him and pleaded for him to let us stay until we finished our final exams at the end of June to graduate, but he wouldn't listen. Our grades were quite good and we couldn't understand why we weren't allowed to finish grade eight. Judging by his facial expression, his mind was made up. He threw all our books into a box and set it outside the school. Then he yelled at us, "Never come back to this school again for neither of you are welcome."

When we stepped outside to catch our bus it had already left. We felt like two living corpses looking for a place to bury ourselves. When it finally dawned on us that we were never coming back to school, we hung our heads in discouragement, and fought the tears that were falling down our faces. We had no choice but to walk the five kilometers home, struggling to carry the box of books together. The question we had was, "Why were we so hated by our teacher?" We tried to think of what we might have done wrong to deserve this. It was difficult to accept the fact that because we were Catholics, we were being persecuted. It was a long way home, but we finally arrived there late in the day. When my mother noticed us coming up the driveway, she approached , anxious to know why we had missed our school bus. She said that when she noticed the bus go by, she had called the school, but the line was busy. When she took one look at our faces and the box of books, she knew for sure that we had received some awful news.

We sat down at the kitchen table and blurted out our frustration and feelings of rejection. After Mom listened quietly to everything we said, she promptly picked up the telephone to call the Catholic School in Oakville. But by mistake she called the wrong school, and got the principal of the public school. Without realizing her error she explained to him what had happened. When she finished speaking, the principal admitted to dismissing us from his school, because we were Catholics and he said that he had no use for Catholics. My mother was quite shocked at his response.

However, rather than argue with this madman, she called the Catholic school and spoke to the mother superior. After finishing her conversation with her, she told us that a bus would pick us up the next day to take us to the Catholic school. Mom happily added, "It's where you all belonged in the first place." My mother was a staunch Catholic and had not liked to see us going to a public school anyway. This experience confirmed her views and feelings. We both passed grade eight with good marks, despite our setback from having to switch schools at the end of the year. We felt relieved that we didn't have to go back to that public school.

Christmas was fast approaching and the steady snow falling left the ground sparkling white and pure. Of course we were happy to see snow fall on the eve of the 23rd when our family went out into the forest to find a large evergreen tree. We chopped it down, dragged it home, and decorated it with homemade trinkets, and popcorn strings. The important thing for the top of the tree was the star, and then to complete the decoration, we put on prickly angel's hair. Finally we stepped back to admire our huge stately tree. All the while, we drank Mom's homemade hot chocolate while we sang a lot of Christmas carols.

On Christmas eve, bathed, our hair curled, and dressed in our best clothes, we attended midnight Mass at the Catholic Church. Once inside the church we all had to genuflect, and make the sign of the cross before we could sit down in the front pews. Soon all six of the children could be found leaning on one another's shoulders, fast asleep until it was time to go home. Tucked in bed, we heard noises coming from downstairs in the wee hours of the morning. Of course, we knew Santa Claus was making the noise as he jumped down the chimney. How surprised he would be to see the oatmeal cookies and glass of milk we'd left on the side table beside the Christmas tree. We flew downstairs to meet "Old Saint Nicholas", but he was nowhere in sight. However, we noticed the cookie dish and milk were empty. Our excitement grew by the minute when we looked under the Christmas tree and saw all those Christmas presents. We knew that this was the best Christmas ever.

Past Christmases had been lean with each child receiving one gift or none at all. However, we could always count on having the most scrumptious Christmas dinner every year.

When Mom heard the commotion downstairs as we all stood around the Christmas tree with our homemade decorations on it, she came down stairs and gave us permission to open our gifts. You could always bank on her to take Kodak photos of us opening our gifts, capturing our facial expressions. After we played with our games, and put back our gifts under the tree, with a feeling of glee, we would bounce back upstairs and delve into our Christmas socks which were tied to the end of our beds. We found Christmas candies, nuts and fruits that our parents couldn't afford during the rest of the year.

Long cold winter nights took on new meaning. After supper and homework completed, we were allowed to go skating on our homemade ice rink. This rink was a labor of love from Mom to us. What a great time we had on our new Christmas skates. We became pretty confident skaters, and enjoyed trying new steps to make skating more fun and interesting.

One Sunday, while we were on the ice rink, my sisters Sandra and Nadine suggested that we play 'crack the whip'. Of course we all wanted to try it. We lined up according to size, and held hands. Everybody had to hold each other's hands very tightly, and couldn't let go, otherwise we could fall, and get hurt. Then the leader, Sandra, would skate fast and pull us in a line around the rink. We never knew when she would stop suddenly and pull the next person's hand really tight, causing the others to fly around in a circular motion. Suddenly, Susan, tripped on her skates and fell on her face, hitting a medium-sized rock. It left her with a big shiner for quite a while.

There was another winter activity that caused a lot of excitement and became a bit risquwe. Some Sundays, my stepfather would tie the toboggan to the back of our old station wagon, and the children including our visiting cousins, would pile on. Then he drove the vehicle very slowly around the long drive way. Sometimes the toboggan would skid too quickly around a corner, and snow would shoot up into our faces. We would just lick it off, and keep shrieking at every turn.

As the end of March approached, all of us were suffering from spring fever. One day Sandra came up with a bright idea. We all agreed that it was the best idea yet to play hooky from school the next day. In the evening, we secretly planned our scheme. That night we could hardly sleep for fear of getting caught. The next morning at the breakfast table, we all tried to act cool, to avoid giving away any clues. With our lunches in hand we waved goodbye to Mom, and walked down the driveway toward the bus stop. We were all together, except for Scamp, our black and white dog. We'd put him in the barn and shut the door so that he wouldn't follow us . We'd left a few minutes early to reach the stop ahead of the bus. As we pretended to wait there, we looked behind toward the house. When the coast was clear, Sandra gave the signal and we all dashed between the evergreen trees and stood as still as statues while the bus rolled up. The bus waited for only a few seconds, then left. During those few seconds we felt a little scared, but our anticipation of the adventure was worth it. Another signal from Sandra, and we all stepped out from the trees and ran as fast as our legs would carry us in the deep snow. We were new at playing hooky, and quite proud of ourselves that we could fool our mother into believing we were at school. Without the evergreen trees near the road to hide between, I don't think we would have succeeded.

Once inside the barn, we sighed and threw ourselves onto the pile of hay. We all felt free as birds and proud as Punch. After continual jumps into the hay we began to get cold and hungry. We decided to eat our lunch and then plan what we should do for the rest of the day. Of course we wished we were sitting in a warm house eating our sandwiches and enjoying a hot drink. We pleaded with my youngest sister, Denise, to sneak into the house and make us hot drinks, and she agreed. After what seemed like ages, Denise came running back to the barn without the drinks. Rather downcast, she said that Mom had seen us sneak to the barn and knew we had played hooky from school. We were told to come into the house, where there was plenty of work to keep us busy all day. Against our better judgment, we reluctantly walked toward the house, dragging our feet.

Inside Mom gave us all a hot drink with our sandwiches before putting us to work. There were piles of ironing to do, beds to make, dishes to wash and the list went on. After ironing the clothes, I walked into the living room for a short break. Just then Sandra playfully grabbed me from behind and flipped me over her shoulder. Since all of us girls were tomboys, it wasn't unusual to enjoy this type of acrobatic display. But guess what happened next? As I came down, my shoulder hit the floor first, and a sharp pain ripped through it. I was lying flat on my back, groaning in pain, when Mom came into the living room. I could tell by her expression that she wasn't pleased with us carrying on like hooligans. At first, Mom thought that I was faking, but when I didn't move, she realized that this was quite serious. The doctor was called and soon on his way. In those days most doctors made house calls, even in the cold weather. After checking my left arm and shoulder, the doctor diagnosed it as a fractured collar bone that would require a sling. How embarrassed I felt when the doctor asked me to take off my heavy sweaters and undershirt. Giggles of laughter came from the hallway. My sisters knew how terribly modest I was. To make matters worse, the furnace had broken down that day and the temperature in the house was cool. As a result of that day, I vowed never to play hooky from school again. It wasn't worth the pain and discomfort I felt for just a short season of fun.

Just a little later, my sister, Nadine, was rushed to the hospital with yellow jaundice and acute appendicitis. Our family's vehicle was broken down, and my stepfather asked my uncle, who happened to be visiting us that weekend, to drive them to the hospital. I felt quite worried about her, especially after a week went by and we didn't hear any news about her recovery.

One evening Sandra's fiancé showed up unexpectedly to visit her. We were all excited to see him. Jack was so tall, dark and handsome with pearly white teeth. Through the course of the evening, plans were made to visit Nadine at the hospital. Of course, I pleaded to go along, arm sling and all. That visit to the hospital turned out to be a disaster. Once there, I smelled a strong ether odor in the corridors that made me feel dizzy and nauseated. When we finally reached Nadine's room, I felt like I was going to faint. I had no idea that I was allergic to ether. When I attempted to ask her how she was doing, I suddenly felt like the room was going around and around. Without warning I fell right on top of her. The last thing I heard was Nadine screaming and yelling at me, "No don't fall on top of me. Get off me." Sure enough I 'd fallen head first right on her stomach and split some of her stitches open. When I came to, I was lying in a hospital bed beside her. I felt like Calamity Jane. It was difficult to look Nadine straight in the eyes about then, for I knew how much pain I'd caused her. I sheepishly went over to apologize. to her, and she managed to grit her teeth, and smile at me despite her pain. I took that smile to mean that she forgiven me. How nice.

Still feeling a little drugged by the ether, I went to get on the elevator that led to the main floor, but the doors shut in my face. Mom, Sandra and Jack went up without me. I was the only one left in the corridor. Finally the elevator came down and Jack walked out quickly, took my hand, and led me on. Mom was tempted to leave me at the hospital as a patient, since her patience was wearing thin.

Winter finally disappeared, Nadine's stomach healed , and my collar bone mended well enough for me to play baseball again. Summer, our favorite season, arrived at last. During the summer months we kept busy building a tree house and putting up a hammock, with Mother's help. When we tired of this, we played baseball with Mom as the pitcher. It was a lot of fun seeing her up front trying to pitch the ball. We had to give a few pointers on how to throw the ball straight. But being a good sport, she stayed with us and found the game a lot of fun.

Our summer included visits from Aunt Gail, Uncle Harry and cousin Larry. They were always part of most weekend events when we were young. No family activities were complete without them. Mom packed a picnic lunch and off we went to our favorite eating spot, the back woods. On a typical outing there, we would observe the giant evergreen trees, and colorful wild flowers. Occasionally, we would spot our province's white trillium set back under some trees. After finding a flat surface in the middle of the forest, we spread the blanket on the ground and proceeded to unpack our picnic basket. When we finished, we all went searching for different leaves in the forest.

One time Sandra whispered, "Look over there ahead of you. There is a snake with her little babies." Sure enough, beside the maple tree was a long slender snake and small baby snakes close beside her. We suddenly stopped in our tracks and kept perfectly still. In fact, we almost stopped breathing, as not to make a sound. The baby snakes started to wiggle and cuddle nearer to mother snake's head. Sensing there were intruders in the forest and that she needed to protect them, mother snake opened up her mouth really wide as the baby snake wiggled towards her. One snake went into her mouth, then others followed, until she had swallowed all five of her babies. Of course, we stood there in sheer amazement wondering if they were in mother's stomach for good, or if they would stay there only until we left.

We were very curious to find out, so we all crept quietly out of the forest area where mother snake was, then we turned our heads to see what she would do. After what seemed like an eternity, she opened her mouth wide and one by one the baby snakes crawled out . "Yucky", we thought. How could she swallow them? Then it dawned on us that the reason she swallowed them in the first place was to protect them from harm. What an object lesson this was for us to discover how nature protected its own creatures.

Quite often, during the summer, we had the opportunity to visit the farm next to us. They had a lot of cows to milk and one bull. One hot sunny morning, I decided to take a little friend with me, a three year old boy who was visiting. We arrived at the barn and visited the cows for a while, then we patted the farm dog. It was time to go home for lunch, judging by the position of the sun straight above us. I picked up the little boy and was carrying him back to the house, when there stood in full view, a black bull, staring straight at us. He started to dig his heels into the dirt. Judging by the saliva dripping from his mouth, I didn't want to hang around to see what he would do next. All of a sudden he came charging after us, and with one quick sweep I put the little boy over the fence, and jumped after him as fast as I could, without looking back.

To our chagrin, summer vacation was almost over, and to add to the let-down, my step- father's company folded up, leaving him jobless. We didn't need a fortune teller to know that another move was on its way. Somehow this move was very different to the previous ones. Very fond memories were to be left behind and we didn't want to give them up just yet. It was a difficult move for all of us, but we tried to hide our disappointment. We were going back to Hamilton, where we'd lived when I was just a little girl. My stepfather found a job quickly, to our relief. Money was needed to pay the mortgage on the house my parents bought. My sister Nadine and I were now in a Catholic high school, and my older sister Sandra had decided to quit school and find a job. The younger children were still in elementary school.

"Joy is not in things. It is in us." Megiddo Message

CHAPTER 7

WEDDING BELLS IN AUTUMN

It was a beautiful day in October, when the maple trees had burst forth with their vivid colors, and strong scents. Autumn has always been my favorite season. This was also the month, back in the sixties, when my Sandra was getting married. She was marrying the man she had dated for eight years, and loved very much. Jack was to be our new brother-in-law. I'd had a crush on Jack when my sister was first going out with him, but it didn't do me any good. He looked like Wyatt Earp, the sheriff on TV. And when he opened his mouth to grin, he had this glowing courgeous Colgate smile. But Jack had eyes only for Sandra, a natural blonde with blue eyes. I used to wonder if blondes had more fun than mousy brunettes like myself.

Jack and Sandra's wedding was a traditional Catholic ceremony in Fort Erie, about a few hours drive from Hamilton. Since our natural father had died two weeks before the wedding, any my mother and step-dad were separated, my uncle Horace walked Sandra down the aisle. He was a chauffeur for Dofasco

Company in Hamilton, and he had permission to borrow the black limousine for the wedding party that weekend. We really felt like we were driving in style. What a impressive car it was. The interior had a red thick carpet along the walls and floor. There was a bar and a TV set that pulled out at the press of a button. I was Sandra's maid-of-honor and Nadine and my cousin were her bridesmaids. Since Fort Erie was where they'd met, they decided to marry there, instead of in Hamilton.

The wedding party stayed at Jack's mother's small wartime house for a week of preparation for the wedding. Jack's mother, Isabel, was a saint of a woman, always doing good for others. With Sandra's permission Isabel instructed us in making the bride's and bridemaids head pieces, made sure the wedding party's dresses were ready to wear, and shoes to match. It's not unsual to find Isabel visiting the sick neighbours wanting to help, or running errands for the neighbours who are shut-ins. She was always at other peoples disposal, even though she had a sick husband and five children to care for. She reminded me of Mother Theresa.

The night before Sandra's wedding, we were all busy doing necessary preparations and we were in need of a break. so my sister, Nadine, my cousin, Alana, and I decided to take a short walk through the town of Fort Erie in the dark. As we were walking and talking Alana noticed that her left foot was throbbing. Upon further investigation, she found something sticking out of her foot. It was too dark to see so we went straight back to the house. There we asked Jack's mother if she could see what was wrong with her foot, and there she found a small nail sticking out of her left foot. The nail came loose with some preying, and Jack's mother cleansed and bandaged the wound. Alana's foot was propped up on a pillow while Isabel begun pampering her.

The wedding day was here at last, and we arose early. Excitement grew like a crescendo, with everyone running in all directions. We hurried to the hairdresser's to get our hair done. After we finished there, our uncle picked us up and drove us home to get ready. There was just enough time to get dressed, since we had to be at the church early for last minute adjustments. We were all ready to depart when we heard a loud crashing noise. My sister and I ran to the bottom of the stairs, and stretched out on the floor was our cousin Alana. She had caught her high heel on a step as she was descending, and had fallen head first down several steps before onto crashing on the floor. Fortunately she was not hurt–she just had a few bruises and scratches, but nothing serious. The missing heel was found intact. Since our dresses matched our shoes, she couldn't just change shoes. We were running late, but someone saved the day by hammering the heel back on. We had just a few minutes to take a quick look in the mirror. Sandra looked just like the actress Princess Grace Kelly in her beautiful white lace, hooped dress. Her cheeks were rosy and her shiny eyes revealed joy.

Finally we reached the church, and scampered out of the limousine to the back door. The rest of the wedding party was in place, and all the guests and family were seated. At the sound of the wedding march, we attempted to walk slowly and gracefully down the aisle. Since we'd rehearsed the night before, we knew how to pace. Our eyes were perched on Alana who was faking a graceful walk down the aisle trying so hard not to put too much pressure on her fragile heel. To our chagrin, the heel had broken off again as she was about to embark down the aisle. We stuck it back on again with a hope and a wish. When the church wedding was over and the register signed, we were relieved that things had gone so smoothly, despite the broken heel. At the reception hall, after the meal was over, the bride and bridegroom had the first dance, then we joined them on the dance floor to music of the sixties. Unfortunately, while I was dancing with my sister Nadine, the priest, who had performed the wedding, came onto the dance floor inebriated, and wanted to dance with us. He could hardly stand up straight, let alone dance. Both Nadine and I managed to pull away from him. After awhile the bride and groom went home to change into their going away outfits for their honeymoon.

"People like trees must grow or die. There's no standing still."
by Joseph Shore

CHAPTER 8
GROWING UP

Through our mid-teens my mother introduced her children to Tarot card reading, tea reading, palm reading, along with Ouija board games, and through the years it became a weekly ritual. Some of us would even read our horoscopes daily in the newspaper, and would believe every word that the astrologer prohesized

All through high school I played the clown in the class room. I attended an all girls Catholic high school. Nuns were usually the teachers and Sister Gertrude was our Grade Eleven Sewing and Geography teacher. She was in her mid-fifties, and hadn't much patience with the youth. There were a few experiences that stand out in my mind that are worth sharing. One day in class Sister Gertrude was talking about the importance of learning Geography during high school, because it would be a practical tool for students later on in life. Well, I wasn't a very strong student of Geography and decided to play the clown by blackening my teeth with some black sticky paper. Of course, I'd make sure to keep smiling at Sister Gertrude so she would notice. Sure enough, halfway through class she pointed me out and told me to see a dentist as soon as possible.

Another time a funny experience happened in Sister Gertrude's sewing class. This time it didn't involved me. We had to wear school uniforms, and every girl in her class had to make a white blouse with a peter pan collar to wear with our navy blue uniform. Sister Gertrude had one of the students demonstrate how to sew the collar to the blouse. As the sewing machine was humming away, Sister Gertrude was bragging about how well this particular girl sewed. Unknown to Sister Gertrude the girl accidentally began sewing her blouse to the cuff of Sister Gertrude's sleeve. Great peals of laughter broke out among the girls when the embarrassed nun discovered what happened.

Previously my sister, Nadine and I, had come out of Home Economics class where we were learning to cook hot dogs. When we entered the sewing room to watch the blouse demonstration, Nadine tried to stick her hot dog into her uniform pocket. But she wasn't aware that it fell to the floor instead. What made it worse, was that Sister Gertrude stepped on it accidentally, and her skinny black-stocking legs flew up in the air as her body came down with a thump. The bell was sweet music to our ears and we ran out of there like we were on fire.

Some things never changed and one such example was our parents on-going arguments, and their resentment toward one other. I felt like a victim of my step-dad. Through the years he would force me to go upstairs to my bedroom and would strap me several times. He always made sure that no one else was upstairs when he did this. One time I asked him, "What did I do wrong to deserve this?"and his answer was always the same," You did nothing wrong, I strap you just in case you do something wrong." As devastating as this ritual became I felt that he was punishing me, because of his resentments toward my mother.

More than once he threatened to kill me when mother was gone to visit her family. Usually when she visited them it was in order to ask them a favour. She was ready to leave my step-dad again, and she needed financial assistance so that Sandra, Nadine, and I would move away with her. Whenever mother left to visit her family it was usually around the time the move would take place, and my step-dad would act out with threats.

On such a night, when my sister and I were in bed sleeping, I woke up to a noise of our creaky bedroom door opening and my step-dad entering. He came toward my side of the bed and knelt down. It looked like he was carrying something in his hand and in a low voice said, "I plan to kill you before the night is through." Then he quickly got up and left the room, closing the door behind him. Of course, I was so petrified that my heart began to race, and I felt an anxiety attack coming on. I began to say some Catholic recited prayers, then finally I closed my eyes, and tried to visualize this man Jesus Christ enveloping me in his arms to protect me from any harm. It was such a relief to wake up the next morning and find myself alive and breathing. There were repeated incidents like this. However, Jesus always kept me safe.

No one had any idea back then just how much I wanted to be rescued from my burdensome life of possible harm and danger. There seemed to be recurring incidences. One time I was around sixteen years old when my mother was working at the hospital, and I was alone ironing some baskets of clothes in the dining room. My step-dad came up to me from behind with a wrench in his hand, and waving it in my face with a stern angry tone said, "You know that you are a stupid idiot and you are lucky to be still alive." Then he pushed me against the wall, and I began to scream, but my siblings didn't hear me yelling. I suddenly realized that my step-dad made sure they were outside playing. Once I was against the wall he kept pushing me hard with his big stomach. At that moment, I realized that I would never want to be overweight like him, and my battle with eating disorder, anorexia bulimia, began until well into my forties. My health was already impaired with stomach ulcers and now I acquired an eating disorder. Several years later as a pastor's wife my sisters Sandra and Nadine confronted me with my eating disorder and told me about their research on the subject. They believed that I was suffering with an eating disorder and needed to seek counselling. They were the first ones to make me aware of it, because I spent several years in denial.

After every meal my habit I would consistently go to the washroom, lock the door, and put my fingers down my throat until I vomited what I ate. As a Christian I was ready to face my demon by pleading daily for God's healing. God is the great Physician, and gradually He answered my prayer and I found myself not giving into my former habit. What a burden was lifted from my shoulders as I became free from such a addictive threatening disease.

Several years later, it was a happy surprise to learn that when I became a converted Christian, that because of Christ and what He did for all of us, on Calvary's cross, Heaven would be incomplete without us when Jesus returns to bring us home with Him.

Finally I graduated from high school along with a secretarial course. My teacher managed to arrange an interview for me with an insurance company in our city. I was so excited when I got hired. Even though I suffered from shyness and low self-esteem, the staff treated me with kindness and respect. I had a lot to learn about office procedures and I was eager to learn all

I could. Gradually I caught on to the routine and felt at home with the staff, but not with the telephones. It was part of my job to answer incoming calls and take telephone messages, but I always seemed to be tongue-tied . There were a few snickers from the office staff, whenever I answered the telephone. I tried not to show my red flushed cheeks, and quivering voice. However, as time passed, answering phones became routine, and I didn't find it a challenge anymore. Every Tuesday evening the entire staff of twenty including myself, would go bowling after work for an hour. This social event brought us closer together. After I'd worked a year at Simcoe Insurance company, the owner and assistant manager purchased another insurance company that was going bankrupt. That meant that the entire staff had to work overtime with long hours for almost a year.

Each fiscal year, the company auditor would check the financial books. One time, the auditor discovered an unaccounted deficit of $5,000. Not suspecting the company accountant of foul play, we would tease him about the missing money. He was a pleasant, pleasant person who seemed to have his life together. However, after further investigation, it was discovered that the accountant was found guilty of stealing the money. He lost his job, and his credibility. The entire staff was taken by surprise when we heard the sad news. We found it difficult to understand why he would jeopardize his job just for $5,000, but we were not in his shoes. The pressures of debts and responsibilities might have driven him to take the money. The last time we heard, he was selling water softeners door-to-door.

"Fame, like flame, is harmless, until you start inhaling it" by O.A. Battista

CHAPTER 9
FASHION MODELING

Spring was in the air and I felt that a hobby would be just what I needed. I was browsing through the newspaper on my lunch break, when an advertisement caught my attention. It mentioned a self- improvement course that would enhance women's social skills, physical posture and self confidence. "I could sure do with some confidence," I thought. Immediately I called to inquire about it and decided to enroll in a course with the fifteen weekly lessons. It proved to be very productive and informative. I soon felt the benefits of this course. I was building confidence in myself, and feeling less shy and awkward when speaking to people. After completing the fifteen lessons, my teacher approached me privately and asked if I would be willing to take modeling classes. She felt I had the talent in this area. Obviously she'd seen something in me of which I was unaware. After much persuasion on the teacher's part, I agreed to try the fifteen modeling lessons.

My decision to take this course changed my life for the better. Things became hectic but exciting. I had the opportunity to do some occasional evening fashion modeling, and keep my full time job at the insurance firm. There were often fashion shows being held in various clothing stores in Hamilton, in which I participated.

One evening I arrived a little early for class. My modeling teacher asked me to sit down, and relax. She had something important to tell me. I blushed and felt a bit anxious wondering if she had changed her mind about my ability to model. It turned out to be the exact opposite. She told me she was entering me in the Miss Hamilton Beauty Contest and wanted me to commence training. Wow! This took me completely off guard and I tried to wiggle out of it, pleading shyness and anxiety, but she would hear none of it. She told me I had a very good chance of winning, and if I didn't enter I would regret it for the rest of my life. Her confidence in me and belief that I could win finally broke down my resistance.

For the big night, I bought an inexpensive, simple yet elegant long aqua green evening gown that fit me perfectly. Since I didn't like wearing long evening gloves I chose not to. Upon arriving at the Sheraton Hotel, I noticed the other fifteen contestants all wore them, and I felt a little conspicuous, wondering if I'd be disqualified from the beauty pageant. When my modeling teacher arrived, she spoke words of encouragement and we joked a little to break the tension. As each contestants name was called, she had to choose a sealed envelope from a basket and answer the question it contained. When my turn came, I picked an envelope with shaky hands and read the question. "Should youth under 21 years of age be allowed to drink?"

After reading the question out loud, I had three minutes to think of an appropriate response. I was uncomfortable, because I knew how minors felt about drinking behind their parents' back. Many of my friends did it, including myself. I was apprehensive to speak my heart felt feelings because this might betray trust with my friends, or create ill feelings with the older generation in the audience. After wrestling with the question, I found myself saying what was on my heart.

"Ladies and gentlemen, I want to be honest with my audience by saying that, if the youth of our generation is old enough to fight in the Viet Nam War, they are old enough to take an occasional drink. I believe older youth should be able to make that personal choice for themselves." There didn't seem to be anyone who wanted to throw rotten eggs at me, so I felt relieved that my point of view was accepted.

In later years, I discovered how harmful alcohol is in damaging brain cells, and decided not to drink any form of liquor. Beer was something hairdressers used on women's hair back then. I felt it was better to have beer applied externally than internally.

After modeling our gowns, the contestants had to wait backstage while the judges tallied the votes. Of course some of the girls asked me the inevitable question of why I wasn't wearing long gloves, and I calmly mentioned that I found the long gloves to be too tightfitting. The final moment came at last, and they called us all up on stage to announce the winners for Miss Hamilton. The second and first runner-ups were called first by the judges. After what seem like an eternity my name was called as the winner of Miss Hamilton. I froze on the spot and my legs felt like rubber. I kept repeating to myself "Is it true? Did I really win the title, or is this just a dream?" It certainly was a grand occasion. I accepted the beautiful red flowers and a trophy, which I still have.

After winning Miss Hamilton I felt much more prepared to enter other beauty contests, including Miss Dominion of Canada. The name has since been changed to Miss Canada. The beauty contest always takes place on July 1 at Niagara

Falls, Ontario. I entered this large contest as Miss Hamilton, with such strong support from my modeling teacher, I just couldn't let her down. It felt like I was doing it mainly for her, instead of for myself.

Out of one hundred girls who applied for Miss Dominion of Canada Beauty Contest, fifteen were chosen, and I was among them.. These fifteen contestants stayed at a luxurious hotel in Niagara Falls for one week before July 1, Canada Day, to see how well they would perform. With a heavy daily schedule, and five hours of sleep a night, needless to say we were worn out by the end of the week. And we still had to face the big finals on Dominion of Canada Day.

During the week we were chaperoned to various meetings held by the mayors of various Canadian and American towns. Our day would start at 5 a.m. and finish at 11 p.m. There were also sightseeing tours in Niagara Falls and New York State. Even though we were weary with exhaustion, we managed to have fun. One of our guides showed us the spot where the actress Marilyn Monroe and actor John Wayne were on a raft while making a movie. He also told us other memorial stories about famous people who visited this honeymoon city. All in all, there were not many chances to relax. Even when swimming in the large hotel pool, the movie cameras gathered around, shooting pictures of us swimming or sitting on lawn chairs soaking up the sun.

One day our agenda included a visit to see the mayor of New York State. While being driven in cars to various functions, we were often escorted by police. An opportunity to snooze in the car was tempting, but the distance was never long enough to gain any worthwhile sleep. This day we were greeted warmly by the mayor and directed to a table where we were to be his supper guests. After introductions were made, the mayor began his speech, and without planning to take a snooze, I leaned my head down on the table. But I quickly fell into a deep sleep. Apparently after the mayor finished his speech, someone nudged me awake. Suddenly I realized where I was, and blushed with shame as laughter broke out all around me. To make matters worse, the mayor asked me to come to the front and give a small speech of my own, since I'd found his so boring. Speechless and embarrassed, I slowly made my way up front. I can't recall my exact words, but I mentioned something about my appreciation for having been invited to come here to meet the mayor, despite my snoozing, while he gave his important speech. This brought even greater laughter from the girls. You can be sure after that experience, I never fell asleep anywhere else, except in my hotel room and at the appropriate times.

As I mentioned before, each girl had a chaperon who never left her side except to use the washroom. But one evening while my chaperon was away, there was a tap on my hotel door. At the door was a girl I'd seen only once. She asked me to come and help her sick roommate. I reminded her that if any of us left our room without permission, we would be disqualified. However, she insisted that I visit this sick roommate. I reluctantly went to her hotel room, and as I entered, I noticed covers were over the sick girl's head. Standing next to her bed was another girl, former Miss Dominion of Canada. They told me to lift the sheet and see who was underneath. As I bent over the bed to do so, there were little giggles in the background. There between the sheets was a mannequin, dressed up in a nightgown and with a wig on her head. Obviously they had set a trap to get me disqualified from the contest. I knew I could lose my chance at winning so I asked the former Miss Dominion of Canada why they'd had done this?

She looked straight at me and said, "I've been wanting to get even with you for sometime, for going out with my boyfriend."

After much discussion we discovered that she'd mistook me for another girl. I wasn't going out with her boyfriend. When my chaperon heard about my leaving the room to visit someone else, she was upset and planned to report me. I told her what had happened and how I sincerely thought that I could help this sick girl. After much thought she decided not to report the incident to her superior. The girls in my room rallied around me, happy to know I could stay. It was a known fact that my chaperone was the mother of the previous Miss Dominion of Canada who had to resign, due to a conflict of interest, and so the second runner up was put in her place.

A few nights before the contest, many of the girls were receiving telephone calls from their families and boyfriends, and some of them received beautiful roses. I guess I was feeling left out and sorry for myself, because I knew my family couldn't afford to call me long distance. At that time, I was dating a student of medicine who wasn't happy that I was entering any beauty contest. My roommates noticed that I didn't receive any flowers, so they played a joke on me. They invented a story about a handsome man delivering flowers for me at our hotel room while I was taking a bath. They were acting too excited, and I had a suspicious feeling that this scenario was leading up to something. Suddenly, the bathroom door swung open as they threw their empty flower boxes into the bath water. It seemed they would never let me forget it. I guess they might have felt sorry for me, and didn't want to leave me out of their fun.

After each full day of activities, we arrived at our hotel rooms late at night. We could hardly wait to take off our make up, our false eye lashes, and wash our faces. There were two double beds in each room and Miss Niagara Falls and I shared one bed. Around midnight, we crawled into bed, dying from fatigue, and were soon sawing logs. Some time during the night our bed broke and we slipped off the edge. Even falling from a broken bed didn't disturb our sleep. We slept on the floor until early morning, when we had to get up and start all over again.

The entire week slipped by quickly, and before we knew it the day that everyone was looking forward to had arrived. Most of us were so relieved to see the end in sight that we didn't care who won the contest. But there were two girls who appeared very tense and worried, because their parents would be more than disappointed if they lost. In fact, their parents had threatened to throw them out of the home, if they didn't win the title. Our hearts went out to them because the rest of us didn't have to worry about measuring up to our parents' expectations.

The night of the contest, we all went about wishing everyone success. After our chaperones made last minute touches to our hair and make up, all fifteen of us formed a single file. Once downstairs, we were lead to the grand ballroom. People started to pile into the hot stuffy room, and the air became stifling. Our smiling faces looked upon the audience. If I'd been a spectator looking at us, I would have thought on the exterior, we appeared poised, and displayed confidence and professionalism. However, since we knew each other, it was obvious we all had the jitters.

When it was time to be introduced to the audience, we ascended the stage in numerical order. Our numbers were pinned to our bathing suits that we modeled. These were one piece Catalina suits, the same green color and a gift from our manager. They fit like a glove and were very attractive and modest. I felt more comfortable in this than in my two- piece bathing suit. The commentator introduced each of us separately, and described the one piece bathing suits we were wearing. After that, we had to model our two piece business suits.

When it was finally time to dress into our long gowns, my chaperon asked me to put on my long-sleeved gloves. I didn't want her to know that my gloves were too small, and I couldn't afford to buy another pair. She wasn't very pleased when I told her I hadn't brought them with me. But I was proud of the gown that my Aunt Anita had made for me. It was a long, sweeping white linen gown down to the ankles, in a Spanish style, and a separate long strip of sheer material attached to the right shoulder. When I walked, the material would float and give me the appearance of a dancer.

The contestant from Newfoundland became especially nervous when it was her turn to go on stage for the second time. Some of us tried to calm her. But when her number was called, she nervously mounted the stairs to the stage, then broke into tears. I felt so sorry for her, knowing how embarrassed she must feel. Her parents had practically forced her to enter the Miss Dominion of Canada Beauty Contest, after she'd won Miss Newfoundland. The manager brought her back to the dressing room where we surrounded her with hugs and encouraging words. It was true that many of the girls parents wanted their daughter to win. They knew that meeting people from all around the world would be a great experience and enhancement to the girls' future careers.

My number was finally called to go back up on stage. Facing me were six judges and a huge audience. With a big smile I looked right at the judges, as we were trained to do. As I was about to do a pivot turn, my heel got caught in a crack on the floor and I couldn't move. What a predicament--I slipped out of my shoe, and yanked it from the crack still smiling, and proceeded to walk the T shaped ramp. It created a stir among the judges and they began to laugh out loud. That was an icebreaker for everyone, including myself. Laughter rippled across the room.

The finale came after the judges had tallied up the scores and discussed their decisions. Then the golden moment arrived. The two runner ups were called and then the new Miss Dominion of Canada from Toronto, was announced. She was one of the girls whose parents would have been disappointed if she hadn't won the title. All of us girls rallied around her, happy that she had won. It was a night which holds many fond memories of close friendships, and high emotions. With mixed emotions and tears of joy, we went back to our rooms to pack.

Contemplating future plans for my life wasn't easy, after coming down from the high cloud where I'd lived for an entire week. Knowing that I didn't want to spend the rest of my life in an office, I decided to travel and work. I was thinking seriously of moving to Montréal and finding work there.

However a few days later I received a call that gave me something to think about. My modeling teacher had a proposition to offer me, and wanted me to take a few weeks to think seriously about it. She proposed that I train for a year as Miss Dominion of Canada, then enter next year's contest. With a lot of training she thought I could be the next year's winner At first I thought this a once-in-a-lifetime opportunity. I promised her that I would give it some serious thought in the next few weeks. There were a lot of advantages to winning Miss Dominion of Canada, including extensive traveling all around the world, competitions in every main country for the title. There were gifts of clothing, luggage, and money, and a possible career in business.

I wrestled hard with my decision and struggled with the thought of losing out on the great opportunities that I could enjoy. Despite my mother and friend's persuasion to train for the title, and compete the following July, I had to be true to my conscience. After the two weeks were over, I called my modeling teacher and gave her my decision not to do this. She was very disappointed to hear me turn it down and begged me to reconsider.

A few days later, I received a call from the previous Miss Dominion of Canada, asking me to go with her to California to explore the possibility of living there. Megan, (not her real name), motivated by her parents would be applying for jobs in the acting field in Hollywood, California. Since I was ready for some adventure , I took her up on the offer.

It was my first time away from home, and I felt a bit scared to launch into a new career in another country. It was also my first flight on a plane and I was quite nervous about flying. In fact, when on the plane my hat slipped half way down my face, I was tempted to keep it there. But when the food was served, I put it back on my head. Once inside the Los Angles airport, we were met by some of Megan's friends. It felt good to have someone greeting us, even though I'd never met them before. What a sight we looked, though, clad in smart dresses, fancy hats and gloves to match, whereas in California most people wore shorts, t-shirts, and sneakers. We were packed like sardines in the small VW convertible, with the wind pounding wildly in our faces and hair. It was the first time I took off my hat after arriving in L.A.

Since Megan knew a lot of people in different parts of California, we stayed with some of her friends for a while. Our first stop was in Malibu Beach where we stayed for a month. One morning I got up early with the sun shining brightly, alluring me to get up. I put on my bathing suit, and ran to the beach. I have never been in an ocean before, and didn't realize how strong and powerful it can be, until I jumped in. A huge wave was coming right for me, and I quickly turned around, rushing to get out of the water. But the wave crashed on my back, and began pushing me under. It did occur to me that I couldn't swim and that no one was around to save me. Finally I came up, caught my breathe very briefly, then was pulled under by another wave, and my feet were knocked out from under me. Down I went for the second time. After what seemed an eternity I was washed to shore. I had thick clumps of sand inside my fingernails, and chunks of it in my long hair.... evidence of my struggles in the vast ocean. I headed to the house without so much as a backward glance.

Our next stop was Hollywood, where we stayed for a few months, touring the city and enjoying the highlights. Then we made our way to Long Beach and stayed with more of Megan's friends for awhile, before finally getting our own apartment in a large apartment building in Bellflower. Our funds were running low, and we were too proud to ask our families for financial help. Therefore, we decided to apply for our Social Security Cards, receiving them within a few weeks. Megan got a job as an airline stewardess flying between L.A. to Las Vegas. Being known as Miss Dominion of Canada from the previous year, helped her land a job quickly. A funny thing happened to her while she was training as a stewardess. She was practicing emergency procedures and when the instructor told her to jump unto the rubber-like slide that leads to the ground, she stumbled and tumbled down the slide, head first. Lucky for her the plane was on the ground.

Another time, Megan came up to a passenger and asked him to fasten his seat belt. All of a sudden he took her by the waist, and placed her on his lap, and tried fastening the seat belt around them both. It was times like these she said, that she wished she had applied for another career.

While I was waiting for my modeling photos to arrive to use for TV commercial auditions, I took a job in an engineering office as a receptionist and secretary.

A week before Christmas, while I was working in the front office, an agent from Texas arrived. I knew from previous experiences, that my boss did not want to see him. Making up excuses on behalf of a boss, isn't always easy or convincing. However, after explaining to the Texan that it was impossible for him to see my boss that particular day, he finally left the office. In the meantime, my boss came into my office with a box of Christmas cheer (bottles of liquor) for me to pass out to each company customer. Then without warning, the Texan man returned to leave his card and telephone number. Quickly I motioned to my boss to hide under my desk, since it was too late for him to escape. What was I to do now? The Texan with the tall hat approached my desk with a big smile, and handed me his card. He stayed and talked about everything under the sun, including the possibility of Canada emerging with the United States one day. What a political conversation to throw at me at nine o'clock in the morning. What a relief to see him leave the office. I quickly peeked under the desk, affirming with my head that my boss could come out of hiding. We both had a good chuckle, with my boss trying to impersonate the Texan's accent.

Letters from back home came regularly, and I faithfully responded. Judging by Megan's letters from her parents, they still wanted her to succeed in the movie industry. So in order to please her parents, she decided to arrange an interview with Universal Studios, and try out for "The Dating Game". She wanted me to accompany her to studios, and while she was auditioning, I sat in the office lobby contented to read a magazine. That's when something unusual happened.

The secretary, who looked the splitting image of the comedian, Phyllis Diller, gave me a form to fill out to audition for The Dating Game. Timidly, I said that I was just waiting for a friend who was auditioning. But she wouldn't take 'no' for an answer, and took a photo of me with a Polaroid camera. She attached the photo to a blank form, and insisted that I write my name and telephone number. Reluctantly, I filled out part of the form, and before I could object, I was gently pushed into a room filled with over fifty girls. Feeling awkward and embarrassed, I sat in a far corner at the end of a bench, hoping not to be noticed. With so many girls wanting to get on "The Dating Game" show, I was sure that I'd never be picked.

Not so. After the producer interviewed my friend Megan, he immediately called my name. At first I didn't respond, but to my chagrin, Megan pointed me out. He asked me to stand up. Slowly I stood to my feet while he threw a few quick questions at me. The producer sensed that I was there against my will, and asked me to come up to his desk. My face turned beet red as he asked me how old I was and where I came from. There were more general questions and finally he announced that was all for the day. I quickly made my way out the door. In the meantime, Megan caught up with me. She knew that I didn't like being put on the spot. Anyway, we felt that the studio would leave us alone, since there were so many other girls who desperately wanted to be on The Dating Game. However, a few days later, Universal Studios called me to have another interview with them. It seemed so ironical that my friend who planned to break into the movie industry, didn't get called, and here I was with no future plans for Hollywood, receiving a call from Universal Studios for an audition. Megan encouraged me to accept another interview. Feeling awkward I reluctantly said yes. After the second interview, with two producers present, I was asked to appear on The Dating Game Show. Knowing how terribly shy I was, I didn't accept their offer, which baffled them considerably.

I realized then how desperately I needed my modeling agent with me. Perhaps it could have made a difference, since she was the only person that could motivate me to reach my impossible dreams. One producer finally said, "There are many girls wanting to try out. Why don't you want to accept our offer?" Since I couldn't tell them how fearful I was of blundering it, and feeling inadequate to perform on TV, I just told them I wasn't interested in being on any T.V. show. Which wasn't true. However, that chapter in my life was quickly over.

My job at Bechtel Engineering was working out quite well, and my new boss was very pleased with my performance, so he gave me a raise after only two months. One day the head office called me from San Francisco asking for my identification number, so it would be legal for me work in the United States. It dawned on me that I didn't have any such number, but I thought of a stall tactic by giving my birth certificate identification number. What should I do next? The heat was on, and feeling guilty, I went to the boss to confess my wrong about the number. But what came next surprised me so much, I broke down crying. When I tried to explain my dilemma, my boss thought that I was unhappy with my raise. Worried that I would quit, he promised me another raise. This took me off guard. I left his office with nothing resolved. My problem was more complicated than before I went to see him. If only I'd had the courage to tell him the truth about my illegal status, perhaps he would have tried to sponsor me to stay in the United States legally.

I resigned myself to the fact that I had to leave the country, quickly, before the law caught up with me. I knew that I didn't have enough money to even buy a ticket to fly home. If I could hang onto this job for another three months I thought, I could buy a plane ticket home to Ontario. About two months later I received another disturbing call from the head office in San Francisco wanting to know what my identification number was. The number I gave them was not valid they said.

Panic-stricken I tried to reassure them that I would get back to them as soon as possible. I needed just a few hundred dollars more to pay for my airplane ticket, but time was fast running out. I went home that night scared and depressed. If I was caught I knew that I'd be deported and let off at the nearest Canadian border, Vancouver, British Columbia, 3,000 miles from home.

Then an idea came to me how I could earn extra money fast. The Manager of the complex where I lived needed someone to clean four vacant apartments before the end of the month. He would pay $25 each. When I approached him, he agreed to let me do it. What a relief, knowing that I could finally fly home, before it was too late.

It was difficult to say good-bye to my sunny California friends. They were like a family to me, but I felt I had no choice.

Once back home Hamilton, Ontario, Canada,, I found an office computer job at York University, in Toronto. I had a two month computer training program to go through first, and then another girl and I shared an office. We had to set up files and feed various university programs into the computer. We also did various assignments for the dean of the University and the professors on staff. After working at York for a year, I was able to set up an interview for my cousin who needed a job. She was interviewed by my administrator, Mrs. Hooker, who was a very loyal and fair with her employees. My cousin was quite happy to be hired for a job in the registrar's office.

There was one incident at work that did disturb me at a lot. In the sixties, homosexuality wasn't out of the closet yet. One day I was in the registrar's filing room searching for a student admission's file for the dean of the university. A female employee who was married with five young children, came into the filing room as I was climbing a medium size ladder seeking to find this particular file. Suddenly she touched my legs and told me how she would like us to be close friends. I froze on the spot, and when I finally found words to speak, I warned her that if she ever touched me again, I would report her to the Administrator. My threat seemed to have worked because there was no recurring incident.

One Saturday we were working overtime registering adult students for evening classes. When it was time to go home, my cousin had a wacky idea that we should take some of the university furniture, like a few benches, a large circular floor type ashtray and the dean's plant. I firmly disagreed with her. We'd just moved into an apartment a few weeks prior, and she felt we needed more furniture. She made arrangements with a friend of ours to pick us up in his pick-up truck . In the meantime, there were a few security guards roaming around the premises checking inside and outside the buildings. Believe it or not, right under the nose of these two security guards, my cousin managed to take the furniture from the building, and lift it into the friend's truck. I had to lie on top of the bench, and try to hide it, and myself, at the same time.

I recommend that no one ever try something as foolish and daring as that. What regrets I had for allowing her to steal things from our employers. What an awful feeling I had in the pit of my stomach when I walked into work on Monday. First of all, the dean's secretary became suspicious of us, when she found out that we worked on Saturday. Secondly, for a few weeks, other employees became suspicious of us, and I really thought that we would lose our jobs. In the meantime, the rumors eventually stopped. My job was going well and I really enjoyed the friendly atmosphere of the university. I was learning a new trade as a computer operator that was satisfying. Yet I still had a strong yearning to travel. I didn't realize it at the time, but I was really trying to run away from my own fears and insecurities.

It wasn't until I began studying the Bible years later, and became a newborn Christian, that it dawned on me that I had tried to escape from my guilt and shame. At last I was able to gain victory in Jesus. Meanwhile, I felt compelled to write Mrs. Hooker a letter to explain how the furniture had disappeared at York University. I asked her forgiveness, and suggested that I pay for it. What a surprise to receive a letter back telling me to forget the incident, since I'd paid the price with my inner turmoil of guilt. Through the Lord's grace and forgiveness, He redeemed and restored me from my sinful act. I also learned an important lesson about not allowing others to influence me to do what I know is wrong. When I surrendered my life to God, I looked hard and deep for the first time, at one particular repetitive weakness that kept poking its ugly head up. I had to face my weakness of allowing others to influence my life, not always for the best, and leaving me feeling guilty and vulnerable.

The job was going well and I really enjoyed the friendly spirit of the university. Learning the trade of a computer operator was satisfying and had some rewards, yet still I had a strong yearning to travel again and run away from responsibilities, rather than solve my problems.

"Travel broadens the mind, flattens the finances, and lengthens the conversation" by Lois Haase

CHAPTER 10
LIVING ABROAD

Wanting to broaden my horizon, after saving some money up, I quit my secure job at York University, and flew to the British Isles for a visit all on my own. Previously, my cousin Pamela and I planned to go together to England, but at the last minute she had to cancel and since I already purchased my flight ticket I decided to go ahead with my plan. My family was supportive of my arrangement, I guess because I was fulfilling their dreams of wanting to travel as well, but their opportunity never came true.

People from my work gave me addresses of some of their friends to look up in England. One couple I contacted in London, had the titles "Lord and Lady". My friends in Toronto had assured me that I would be tempted to stay longer than planned. My intentions were to spend a few months in England and a few months on the continent. Upon arriving at Heathrow Airport, I started to have second thoughts about visiting that long in a foreign country. Even though I spoke the same language as the British, (at least I thought I did), some of the phraseology was quite foreign to me. I had no relatives or friends to stay with and felt completely alone. Flagging down a taxi the day of my arrival in London was a financial learning experience. The cab driver knew that I was at his mercy and overcharged me. Subsequently, I quickly learned the value of the currency.

After being immersed in the various accents of people while touring the city, I began to sound like a Londoner. In fact, London felt like home to me, even though it didn't resemble my own country. The history seemed to jump out and embrace me everywhere I went sightseeing. Learning history at school wasn't half as interesting as experiencing it and walking on the actual grounds where it was created.

One day I met two girls, older than me, who were visiting from Georgia. We became instant friends. All three of us decided to share a room in a hotel, while we remained in England. We rented a car and toured parts of England and Scotland. What a great tour that was, visiting various places like the Cotswold Hills where the sheep grazed. Mind you, we had no intentions of visiting sheep in the pastures that day, but our car went off the road, barely avoiding an on coming vehicle. My friend Jeannie had a difficult time driving on the opposite side of the road. Driving on the opposite side of the road was indeed a bit risqué for any foreigner.

The first evening we arrived in Newcastle, on the border between England and Scotland, we were all tired and ready for a good night's sleep. We checked into a hotel which resembled a castle. It had a somber appearance about it, along with an atmosphere of mystery and suspense. We planned to stay three nights, wanting to explore more of the area. A hotel maiden took us to our room. It was located in a far corner of the hotel, overlooking beautiful rolling green hills with luscious trees. The girl had a charming Scottish brogue and she made our room comfortable. The beds really looked inviting. She said she would wake us, with a spot of tea before we got out of bed the next morning, as was the English custom. Thanking her, we continued to explore the huge room and small closets. Finally, out of sheer exhaustion, we decided to call it a night and flopped into bed.

Halfway through the night I was startled from my sleep, and felt an eerie presence. I tried to call out to my girlfriends in the next bed, but my frightened voice was barely a whisper. Then I heard some rattling noises near the door which made me jump from my bed. Jeannie's mother had passed away in the States, before Jeannie came to London, and she was still grieving her loss. Suddenly she bolted up in bed, and began talking to her mother as if she was actually in the room. By that time the hair on my arms was standing straight up. Finally, the other girl, Jean, was awakened by the loud talking and realized what was happening. After shaking her friend, Jeannie, she woke up puzzled and confused. We all sat up awake the remainder of the night, talking about the incident and the eerie noises we were hearing. According to us, the hotel was haunted.

The next morning the hotel maiden came into our room carrying a tray with cups of hot tea. We were dressed with bags packed before the tea could get cold. To think we had wanted to stay two more nights.

Finally arriving in Edinburgh, Scotland, we found ourselves in the middle of a Scottish parade and had to wait forever to get out of the traffic jam. But surely this was the most beautiful street in the world-Princess Street. How colorful the Scottish kilts looked as the Highlanders triumphantly played their melodious bagpipes. They were very proud to play their national anthem. We spent a week visiting different parts of magnificent castles and museums in Scotland.

Since we were there between Christmas and New Year's, we decided to take in a ballroom party at the hotel across the road. We met some very friendly Scottish people and enjoyed the evening immensely. Later on we were invited to a small, quaint house party, where it was quieter and pleasant to visit in small groups. The next day, a young gentleman knocked on our door. He introduced himself, before mentioning that one of us left a pair of leather gloves at his house He'd come by to return them. What a gentleman, to take the time to return a pair of leather gloves which happened to be mine.

We thought it less stressful to return to England by rail rather than drive a rented car. So after handing back the car and keys, we bought tickets to board a train for London. Once again my funds were running low, and I planned to look for work to pay my return flight home to Canada. How could I anticipate that it would take an entire year to save the money?

"Things never go so well that one should have no fear, and never so ill that one should have no hope" (A Turkish Proverb)

CHAPTER 11

THE CHASE

After a few futile attempts to find office work in London, I decided to try my luck at modeling. One day after an interview for a modeling job, I was returning to my hotel, when I noticed a set of eyes staring at me from across the street. I ignored the person and kept walking. But to my surprise, he came toward me to ask where a certain street was. He was a tall man, medium built, brown hair, blue eyes, and appeared to be in his mid-thirties. I took my well-worn London street map from my purse, opened it and he gazed at it. Then he noticed a Canadian maple leaf on my coat and asked me, how long I'd been in London. I told him a short while. He said his name was David and he came from Cardiff, Wales. His accent was similar to the Welsh owners at the Inchmont Hotel where I was staying. Climbing the steps to the Inchmont Hotel, I noticed this same man following me. I was somewhat suspicious of him, but I knew that I couldn't stop him from entering the hotel. The manager came up to him and they spoke in their Welsh dialect. But, as I was going upstairs to my room, David proceeded to follow me. What a relief when the owner called out to him to come downstairs. Once in my room I explained to my room-mates how this stranger had tried to follow me to my room, without an invitation. Kidding, they said, "Oh well, there goes your last chance at finding a bloke, (guy)."

We had a little tradition each night whereby we would take turns providing supper. After deciding what little snack we wanted, the one in charge would go to the nearby stores and buy the items, including apple cider or wine. That evening it was my turn. As I was walking towards the busy intersection ready to cross the street, to the stores, that same fellow came up to me and without a word grabbed my arm. Startled by his behavior, I began wiggling out of his grasp. But he had a tight grip on my arm and pulled me close to him. I started to yell and scream for help, but no one would come to my rescue, not even the nearby bobbies, (policemen). Then he hailed a taxi cab, threw me in ahead of him, and gave the cab driver an address. My mind and body were frozen with fear. Time seemed to stand still. I repeated the words over and over that I was being kidnaped, and imagined the worst scenario possible.

The taxi driver kept driving for what seemed an eternity. I couldn't recognize any of the buildings we were passing. My fear mounted even more. I started to plead with the stranger to let me free, promising him the little bit of money I had in my purse. He just grinned and told me to settle down and enjoy the ride.

Finally the taxi came to a halt. The stranger half dragged me out of the cab and pushed me down a set of cement stairs leading to a disco joint. My legs were like putty and my mind like mush as I reluctantly descended the narrow stairs. One glance inside this dark, dreary dungeon told me it was not a place for me. The smell of marijuana and loud rock music permeated the air. People sat around tables looking like resurrected mummies from Egyptian tombs.

In the back part of the disco was a gambling casino. With a tight grip on my arm, this beastly man led me there. He pushed me down on a stool and said to hand over my money. This entire scenario seemed like a nightmare. But I felt some relief knowing that early that morning I'd put most of my money in the hotel vault. I had only $80.00, a few travel checks and my passport in my purse. Reluctantly, I handed over some of the money which he gambled and lost.

Frantically trying to plan a way of escape, I came up with an idea. I told the man I needed to visit the loo, (washroom). Eyeing me suspiciously, he warned me that if I tried to escape he would catch up with me. In my most convincing voice I told him that I'd wouldn't do such a thing. I took my time walking to the washroom, in order not to arouse suspicion. Once inside I quickly stepped onto the sink and opened up a window. The window wasn't too far from the ground, so I climbed out easily.

By now it was quite dark outside and I knew how worried my friends would be. I hoped that they would call the police to report a missing person. I didn't know in which direction to run. There was a main street with a lot of traffic which I decided to take, since it was well lit. Panic-stricken I ran up the street, with no idea where I was going. It was after eleven at night and my body was fatigued and sore.

As I crossed a side road I heard fast footsteps close behind. I refused to admit that it could be him catching up to me. Then in the dark night, a clammy hand reached out and grabbed my wrist. I started to scream loudly, but no one was there to hear.

"It's him again," I groaned desperately to myself. It was the same stranger, who called himself David and had kidnaped me earlier in the day. Despair and agony overwhelmed me. There's a song that I learned since this experience that goes like this:

'Woe despair and bitter agony, deep dark depression, excessive misery. If it weren't for bad luck I'd have no luck at all, woe, despair, and bitter agony'.

He was very vexed and swore at me many times for running away from him. My mind was whirling around with disconnected escape plans. My fear was mounting. Of one thing I was sure, if I didn't come up with a concrete plan soon, he was going to do something very abusive. I knew that my life could be in real danger, but didn't know what to do.

I sensed that he had taken strong drugs, since I noticed his eyes were glossy, his mind was confused, and his speech very slurred. At one point he tried to pull me into some bushes and push me to the ground. I scratched his face with my long nails as hard as I could. He let go of me then, to cover his face, and I ran across the heavy-round- about traffic circle. A few cars stopped. Others missed me by inches. One driver yelled, "Do you want to get killed?" To which I replied, "It would be better than what I am going through right now."

I darted across another street, and the chase was on again. I knew the stranger would be angrier than before, if he caught me. At one point, my high heeled shoe flew off, slowing me down some. I vowed I would never wear high heeled shoes again. I threw my other shoe off and continued running barefoot, gaining momentum. When I dared to glance quickly behind me, there he was right on my tail, only inches away. His face twisted as he gave a devilish smile. He threatened over and over to rape me. I tried to act composed on the outside, but on the inside, I was screaming and crying for freedom from this mad man. Gradually an idea came to me, so I just slowed down and let him catch up to me.

Not far away was a small café, and a flicker of hope inside of me sparked a strategy that I knew I had to try. When he started to give me alternatives, I complied knowing that I had some plans to offset his. I began to act discreetly interested in his plans, but letting him know how great it would be if we could sit down in a restaurant first to talk things over. He agreed to go to the restaurant, but warned me that if I tried to run, he would catch up, and my life would be over.

Once inside the restaurant I noticed the Italian owner was putting chairs upside down over the tables. He was closing up for the night. Quickly, I sat down at a table and ordered two cups of coffee. David sat close beside me-not wanting me to get away again. When the coffee came, the owner told us that his restaurant was closing very shortly. I knew that this was my only chance to be free. I slowly got up, and followed the owner to the cash register, muttering something about paying for the coffee. As I paid for it, I began to cry, and with a choking voice I said, "Please sir, help me. This stranger at your table has kidnaped me and held me hostage since early evening. Here is my passport to prove that I am a visitor from Canada." At that point I couldn't stop shaking, as I begged him to call the police. He glanced carefully at me, then without saying a word he checked my passport. Repeatedly, between sobs, I begged him to help me. He looked at me for what seemed like an eternity. Finally he said he would help me.

The big, strapping Italian walked firmly toward our table, and yelled, "Out". He also threatened to call the police if David didn't cooperate. David began to use foul language and left. I breathed a sigh of relief, as I, at last, had somebody that believed me.

The restaurant owner and his sister drove me back to my hotel. Even though I didn't know God personally then, I found myself thanking Him for watching over me. I shivered at the thought of what could have happened .

After my girlfriends left London to travel back to the U.S., I felt completely alone with the haunted memories of this horrid kidnaping episode. For several weeks I had frightening dreams. Since most of my money was spent, I had to find a job to save up for my return home.

About three weeks later I got an interview with a publishing firm on Fleet Street, the very street where Charles Dickens, the famous old English writer and reformer lived as a youngster. After my final interview the chief editor asked me, "Do you know how to make proper English tea?" To which I replied,

"I am sure I can learn the art of making proper tea-I'm a fast learner". I guess he liked my answer, because he offered me the job of secretary to the chief-editor. My heart skipped a beat as I left the office. It was a relief to know that I could now plan my future and that was to save enough money to return home.

When I left the publishing building after my interview, there was a gypsy man standing on the street nearby. He approached me and my skin started crawling, as I recalled what I'd just gone through with another stranger a few weeks before. This gypsy man was a palm reader and wanted to read my hand. He claimed he could tell the future for me. I quickly shook my head; 'no thanks', and walked away as fast as I could.

A few weeks later, some friends and I were eating in a restaurant, when the same gypsy man came up to our table, and asked to read our hands. I gasped in surprise, as I recognized him. Since the girls reluctantly decided to have their hands read, I thought there would be no harm in doing the same. We were safe in a crowd. When it was my turn to have my palm read, he examined it without uttering a sound. He didn't seem to have too much to say about my future at first. After he thoroughly traced every possible line on my left hand, he slowly moved my thumb back and forth. Finally he told me about my childhood, and some of the challenges I'd experienced. He told me exactly how many siblings I had, including the sisters and brother that were lost in the house fire.He went into a lot of accurate detail about my past. He described my personality and told me I was a strong willed woman with a persevering mind. By moving my left thumb up and down and sideways, he determined that I was a survivor who didn't give up easily. The palm reader also told me that I would marry and unfortunately would have two miscarriages, but that I would at last have one healthy baby. Several years later, I married and eventually had two miscarriages, and one healthy baby just like the gypsy foretold. All of this information he discovered from my palm and one strong left thumb.

The following week, I started my full time job at the publishing firm, which I enjoyed. I learned quickly how much creative planning went into publishing a magazine monthly with articles involving civil engineering and heavy duty machinery.

There was a funny incident that happened in the office. I was informed by my chief-editor that one of their British customs was that the office had two tea breaks. I also found out that it was mandatory. One of my duties was to make proper English tea, twice a day, remember, and clean up afterwards. Since it was my first day on the job, after the tea break I piled the cups and saucers in a tray and quickly asked one of the editors where I should wash the dishes. With a glitter in his eye he gave me directions where to go. However, his directions led me straight out the office front door unto the street. At that moment my chief-editor was entering the building and immediately asked me where I was going with the dirty dishes. Then I realized that the joke was on me.

Life began settling down quite nicely for me and my savings were adding up ever so slowly. It was very difficult to save money, because the pay was so minimal, and rent for a flat or apartment, was so high in London. I mentioned to my Jewish girlfriend that I need a weekend job in order to save extra money to visit the continent with her. She then suggested that I talk to her boss at the café where she worked. Fortunately, he gave me a job as a waitress on weekends. The duties were to wash the dishes, be a short-order cook, and serve the customers. This seemed like a tall order for someone who never had any experiences as a waitress.

One Saturday a customer ordered 'welsh rabbit' and hot tea. I ran into the kitchen looking for a frozen rabbit in the refrigerator, but couldn't find anything that resembled one. When my girlfriend came into the kitchen I asked her quickly where the 'welsh rabbit' is. She pointed to the already prepared bread with cheese and sliced tomatoes on top. It was to be warmed up on the grill before serving it. I thought to myself, "That's what welsh rabbit looks like." Finally, I gave the order to the patient customer who said, "I bet you thought I wanted a real cooked rabbit." How did he know?

Within six months I saved enough money to take a short trip to the continent before returning home to Canada . I took advantage of the warm sunshine and beaches in Italy. What a treat after the fog and rainy days of London.

"It's a strange and tragic truth that spiritual things can be unlearned." by Art Glasser

CHAPTER 12

THE NEW AGE

About a week after I arrived home, I had a job interview with an administrator at York University. I had previously worked there and was fortunate to land another job in a different department, at a decent monthly wage.

In one night my entire life changed. A couple of friends called me up and asked if I would like to go dancing with them that evening. I wanted to decline the offer, but ended up going anyway. It was apparent that my heart wasn't at the dance hall, but I didn't really know where it should be. After sitting at the table, and thinking to myself, "I don't care if I dance tonight or not," The atmosphere of the club was encircled with clouds of smoke. Suddenly, I looked up and saw a man who caught my attention. He stood out in the crowd. His wholesome appearance revealed peace and enthusiasm for life. There was a serenity about this man that I needed. Yes, he really stood out in a crowd. For some reason I was attracted to him, and he I guessed him to be in his early forties. He came towards me, and when he asked me to dance, I took up his offer. After the dance he asked if we could sit down and talk, and I agreed. I surprised myself by opening up my feelings concerning my health problems. Then I mentioned that I would like to quit smoking. Hans was his name. Originally from Germany, he moved to Canada twenty years ago. He was a guru (a spiritual teacher of Hinduism). I was strongly attracted to what Hans had to offer.

This encounter with the New Age came at a low period in my life, when I was subconsciously searching and thirsting for truth, and escape from a suffering world. Hans furnished me with all the Yoga Philosophy books, along with Transcendental Meditation and Occult material. For many people Hinduism, Occult and the New Age all go hand in hand. Having no intimate Bible knowledge, nor knowing about the existence of Satan with his manifold manners of drawing people to himself, I like so many was an easy target. This kind of gullible ignorance can lead many to open to accepting the Antichrist on the assumption that he must be the real Christ.

I soaked up these books like a sponge. I was ready for a new life with a different path, from the one I was heading down. As I began to study the philosophy behind the occult, there was this strong urge within me to drink deeply of this well of knowledge, which promises release from the bondage from the body. Along with the philosophy of the occult, I was shown how to become a strict vegetarian. Then I learned the Hatha yoga exercises which I eventually taught. As I began to feel the peace and security within me, my depression slowly left me. My entire life was absorbed into the New Age Movement. I didn't have any desire to keep in touch with my family anymore, for I'd replaced them with the inner voice who controlled my thoughts and life. I also joined a spiritualism class at the request of my guru. He said it would give me more insight and enlightenment into the spirit kingdom. For three whole years I became a slave to this gentle, but firm voice within me.

I'd grown up in a home environment where Tarot card reading, tea reading, palm reading, astrology and Ouija board games were part of everyday life. I now can see how this smorgasbord of evil devices led me straight into Satan's world. His trap was subtly set until I became his.

Later, Hans became my personal guru and he further replaced my need to communicate with my family by his constant control over my life and through his manipulative devices which were to keep me very active and involved in various spiritist groups. One time I said to Hans, " I would like to take some time to visit with my family. I've been so involved in all of these new groups you have signed up for me that I'm neglecting my family to which is response was, "Don't forget I am the groups you belong to are your family now, your own family don't understand your new spiritual life, so it's better that you have as little contact with them as possible." The New Age fragments families. After all, when one has a guru, who needs family? My main goal in the New Age was to obtain the highest level of god-oneness with the unity of the universe.

After a year I became a Hatha Yoga teacher (Hatha means half moon-half sun). Each morning at 4 a.m., I would get up and do the Hatha Yoga exercises. After an hour of easy breathing exercises, I would then concentrate on meditating on the center light in the middle of my forehead. The main goal was to focus on this center point to eventually free my spirit from the dark carnal body which was in bondage. This spirit, once released, would travel to the spirit world to comfort other spirits.

Many nights I was awakened early by a persuasive voice telling me to get out of bed and perform transcendental meditation by sitting in a lotus position on the floor, and focus my thoughts on the third eye in the center of my forehead. Apparently, the third eye is where the tunnel illumination is located, and concentration on this center part of the forehead is suppose to enable you to communicate with the master guru of the universe found worthy of his presence.

My health habits radically changed during this time. Hans taught me how to be a vegan. Vegetarianism was new to me, and I had no idea how to cook this kind of food. I was a complete vegetarian, eating mainly uncooked vegetables, fruits, and no dairy products. After a quick feed of sunflower seeds and fruits, I would juice some carrots, a piece of beet and celery sticks together. This served as my breakfast. Then after showering and dressing I would be off to work. Following work, I would walk 5 kilometers home rather than take a subway. For supper I would eat a baked potato and a large salad. After I cleared the dishes, I would go into my bedroom and meditate for an hour. Sometimes I would feel a warm glow come over me, sensing that a spirit from another world was trying to give me a message. I would try to listen carefully for any message. I always looked forward to myNew Age Spiritualist meetings each Wednesday and Sunday, because it was a small group of people that included me and treated me like family. Our meetings involved channeling of the dead spirits. There was a cassette recording of a masculine guru who would instruct us to close our eyes and meditate on the third eye in the center of the forehead. Strangely enough he would quote some Bible texts that I don't recall off hand. Then as our eyes were shut Bertha, our Channeler would turn off the cassette and inform us with these words, " An Indian woman from India carrying a small baby in her arms just entered our room. Her baby is physically ill and in need of a healing, so she was called by the Channeler to bring her baby to our meeting for a healing, and how happy I am to announce that a miracle took place right here in this spiritual meeting."

My family of New Agers, substituted my natural family. The occult approach is so deceptive and powerful that it gradually convinced me that I didn't have a biological family anymore- at least not worth thinking about or contacting. My daily routine was very rigid and demanding. The spirit world was controlling my life, and I had no empathy for human suffering and poverty. People who were not of my narrow minded world did not count to me. I became self centered and proud of what I was accomplishing. After all, I thought, who else is as disciplined and knowledgeable about spiritual things as me? Who was as dedicated as I was to rise at 4 a.m. to meditate for long periods of time before going to work? I began to be spiritually proud and a self-acclaimed authority on the spirit world. As my heart delved deeper into the New Way, I had no tolerance for church religion. Slavery is a mighty tool of Satan which kept my life occupied every minute of the day doing his will.

One event I recall was when a medium from the spirit world woke me during the wee hours of the morning, about 2 a.m. and told me to catch a bus to downtown Toronto. The voice continued to give explicit directions as to where to meet a group of New Agers waiting in a van parked on a main street in Toronto. I obeyed the voice and waited for a bus that would take me to the van. The warm air and peaceful silence made me feel calm and relaxed. The bus dropped me off on a main street in Toronto, and it wasn't very long before I noticed a blue van parked up the street, just as the medium had described.

I proceeded toward the van and knocked on the passenger door. When I introduced myself and told him what spiritual group I belonged to he let me enter the van. There were about ten youth including me, who were directed to go to Detroit,

Michigan to attend a large conference. The guest speaker was the wise guru of the famous prophet, Yama Handi. He'd served his master Yama Handi faithfully until he died. We were eager to meet this sage master of the spirit world, in hopes he would pass along his techniques and experiences.

Finally, we arrived in Detroit and quickly piled out of the van. Entering the building, we were surprised to see hundreds of people crowding into the auditorium. To think we came an hour early to find a good seat. Our small group of ten barely got a seat at the back of the room. After some brief announcements about the guest speaker, the master guru rose to his feet and seemed to glide to the microphone. His strides seem so effortless when he walked. He actually didn't need a microphone for his voice flowed like ripples of water in a stream. He had a faraway look and appeared to be in a trance. From time to time during his talk, he indicated that when he paused, it was because he was receiving messages from the spirit world for certain people in the audience. He passed on these messages as they came. We sat spellbound and struck by his powerful deportment and spiritual wisdom. His main theme and message to us was, "Dear children never let go of this new light. Discover all that the inner conscious can reveal. Tap into your source of oneness with the spirit medium."

His message bore a lot of weight on the audience; we felt regenerated and revitalized. Right there, I committed myself to a stricter lifestyle with longer periods of meditation with the inner conscious that could free me from the bondage of the carnal world. The master guru was at the back of the auditorium shacking hands with everyone as they left. When it came my turn, he told me he had a positive message to share with me. His pensive dark brown eyes stared deeply into my soul. It sent a shiver up my spine. His words went something like this, "Keep striving to achieve the ultimate freedom from the bondage of the body. Listen carefully to your inner voice, and it will direct you to a higher plane of greatness and oneness with the universe." Literally, I floated to the van, after his encouraging message. On our way back to Toronto, the ten of us became quick friends, uniting together in the brotherhood of the New Age Movement. I was surprised to discover that one of the girls had been an actress in the Broadway musical,"Hair" in London, England.

On occasion I'd believe that the spirit world was transmitting certain dreams to me that I thought I could interpret. For instance, when my friend's father was dying, I had this dream that he was bleeding to death. The next day my friend called to say his father died of kidney failure. My immediate response was that I had a dream of her father dying. It was these strange interpretations that made me feel very important and all wise, like a prophet.

At our New Self-Realization meetings, we would listen to tapes by spiritualists speaking to us about spirits leaving the body to join other spirits in the spirit world. We would close our eyes while the lecturer was speaking, and slowly our minds would drift far way in a trance. My teacher was a medium who allowed herself to be a spokes person for the spirits. You can imagine what kind of evil spirits were visiting our small group from time to time. Once, while our class was sitting in the lotus position in a deep trance, try as I might to open up my eyes, I couldn't. My eyes felt weighed down. I heard a faint tap at the door and I sense that someone entered the room. I became anxious to see who that person was, but I couldn't open up my eyes. At the same time I felt a presence beside me, as a hem of someone's clothes brushed past my arm. Finally our medium told us to open our eyes, and mine opened automatically. Remembering what I'd heard and felt, I looked quickly around to see if there was a visitor in our midst, but there were no new faces. Our teacher explained to us that a girl from India, carrying a small child had come into our presence seeking healing for her baby. Of course I accepted her answer, and felt so proud to be part of a healing group.

The curtain of my life gradually began to descend, as signs of illness took over. It happened as I was reaching the peak of my career and success with teaching yoga exercises. At that time I was working with a large advertising company as an assistant advertiser of TV sports. My job was to buy spots on TV for sports and other commercials. I was being trained by two gentleman who had been in this line of work for over twenty years. My plans for my work and personal life were fitting together so well that I thought nothing could disrupt them. But gradually, I began having terrific headaches with frequent nausea and vomiting spells.

Even though I'd been a strict vegetarian for almost three years, my health seemed to be slowly deteriorating. I had a very sore neck with a lot of stiffness and no mobility. Trying to find the cause, I visited one doctor after another, but their answers were the same. No signs of neck damage showed up on the x-rays. At first I took a lot of prescription pain killers. But I seemed to be suffering a lot of side effects. So I finally threw them out. As my problem became critical, I knew I couldn't last much longer without immediate help.

In the end, I had to give up my job temporarily, a job of which I was very fond. I had to miss many of the New Self-Realization classes which met twice a week. I felt so ill that I also stopped reading material on the occult and other New Age books temporarily. My life was on hold, and I began to feel anxious and unsure of my future.

When my channeling teacher heard that I was becoming quite sick, she arranged for me to see Kathryn Kuhlman of California, the great spiritual healer, who was visiting Toronto

Sport's Stadium. I couldn't find the stadium, and as a result, wasn't healed. I returned home defeated, depressed, and discouraged. While sitting in my rocking chair feeling sorry for myself, my thoughts went to a superhuman being, and I wondered how he viewed me as a person. At that moment, my main concern was whether or not this impersonal God loved me. That was the first time I seriously thought of the possibility that I might die and what would happen to me after death. As I sat rocking in my chair, there appeared in front of my face, a slender right hand with the top piece of the index finger missing. This vision of a hand brought me reassurance and peace. Somehow with the little faith I had, I believed God would heal my neck.

A few days later there was a knock on my door. It was my channeling teacher;a channeler is someone who communicates with dead spirits. She was concerned about my health to the point that she'd made an appointment with a chiropractor friend to see me. Since I felt so weak and discouraged about my health, I went along with her. He was not only an amazing ninety-four year old chiropractor, but also a strong Christian believer.

When he adjusted my neck, he explained to me that my two upper neck disks; the axile and axis were slowly dislocating, and I wasn't receiving much oxygen to my brain. I don't know how true this was, but he said that I was heading for a small brain tumor, if I hadn't had the problem corrected. To my amazement when I saw this Christian chiropractor's right hand, it was the same hand with the missing top piece of one finger I'd seen in my vision.

My neck was healing quite nicely and there was full range of motion, with no pain. One day, when I was having a treatment, the chiropractor mentioned that he was a Baptist Christian. He shared with me several stories about Christ intervening in his life, when he was in a lot of danger as a pilot during the II World War. Later on he invited his patients, including me to tea at his apartment after my treatment.

He wasted no time opening up his Bible to I Corinthian 15:51-55 . This text speaks about our corruptible body putting on the incorruptible body. To be honest, I felt very uncomfortable listening to the Bible. What I know now, that I didn't understand back then, was the evil spirit in me strongly disliked the Holy Spirit dwelling in this Christian's heart. The very subject that Satan didn't want me to know about was that the dead in Christ will be transformed from death unto newness of life. Our sinful and weak bodies will be changed into strong, pure Christ-like bodies. Because the Bible did away with my belief in reincarnation, I became inwardly angry, so much so, that I stopped going to see this Christian chiropractor. I kept telling myself that the Bible was just a fiction story book, and I convinced myself that I really enjoyed attending my Self-Realization Classes in Channeling more.

I had to admit though that there were parts of these sessions that were scary. During the group meditation we students were encouraged to focus on the 'third eye', and I was put into a deep, deep trance, while trying to concentrate on my mind leaving my body. One time in particular, when I was in a long trance, I feared that I'd never come out of it. When I finally did come out, it was such a relief to discover that I was still in my body.

One night, after a session of channeling, my teacher told me that she had a dream about me the night before. She explained that I was going to join a Protestant church, and that I would meet and marry a wonderful Christian gentleman who would become a strong dedicated minister. At that time it was the last thing I wanted to hear, and told her so. To my astonishment, everything about the dream that my channeling teacher had told me came true. I eventually became a Seventh-day Adventist Christian and married a minister. I believed that God revealed to my teacher His plans for my future.

"Never, for sake of peace and quiet, deny your own experience or convictions." by Dag Hammerskjold

CHAPTER 13

AT CROSSROADS

As I mentioned previously I didn't have much contact with my family while in the New Age since my guru discouraged family visits. Also at that time, I wasn't aware of my mother's new found faith in Jesus, and her baptism into the Seventh-day Adventist Church. Just after her baptism my mother started to visit me on weekends. She lived in Hamilton, about an hour away from where I lived in Toronto. What surprised me about her visits was that she carried a Bible with her and read it quite often. Knowing that she'd attended the Roman Catholic Church all her life, it seemed unusual to see her carrying a Bible. I wanted nothing to do with it and avoided any discussion about religion. My mother knew I was firmly set in my own lifestyle, and especially committed to the New Age. She was wise enough not to mention anything about her new found Christian faith. I even invited her to my New Age class, hoping to convert her to the New Age so that she would be distracted from the Bible. She accepted my invitation, but before leaving for my class, she tucked her Bible under her arm. This disturbed me a lot, but I didn't voice my displeasure. Once the class was in session and the speaker on the tape was talking, the members of the group would go into a trance like state, all except my mother, who was keenly observing us in the background.

Following our session, my channeler teacher invited us all to sit around the table for a cup of tea and baked goods. We would all sit around and discuss what the speaker had said. It seemed that a Bible text was always quoted by the speaker, but also many different quotes from various authors. However, Mother caught some of the Bible texts the speaker quoted on his tape, especially the text concerning the Ten Commandments being nailed to the cross. I could feel my cheeks blush, as I nudged her foot with my foot under the table to signal her to stop talking about the Bible. After a brief discussion on the cross, I excused myself by muttering something about having to go right away. Outside, Mom could see by the look on my face how disappointed I was. She patiently changed the subject and spoke about other things. Soon the matter was dropped.

It seemed after each weekend my mother had visited, there were new spiritual booklets left on the table. I pretended not to see them and went about my routine. One morning before leaving for work, I noticed the title of a booklet that interested me. So I threw it in my purse, and went to work. On my lunch hour I scanned the booklet briefly, then settled down to read it. Again feelings of irritation welled up inside of me after reading this booklet, written by George Vandeman about what happens when someone dies. I threw it back in my purse vowing never to read it again.

My vacation was quickly approaching and I planned to spend a week with my friends in Ottawa. The remainder I'd be at my mom's new place in Hamilton. The weekend before my vacation started was so sunny and warm that I brought a few books and a blanket to the backyard of the house where I was staying. I spread out my blanket on the lawn and proceeded to get comfortable. There were also a few other girls who rented there, sitting in the backyard. We chatted a little before I settled down to read.

As I was nicely getting into reading one of my New Age books, a strong thought came to my mind that urged me to go see my mother who had just moved into her new place in Hamilton. I ignored this voice and proceeded to read. But the impression grew stronger to go visit my mother. Again I ignored the thought. Time and time again, this same thought would go through my mind and wouldn't give me any rest. Without realizing what I was doing, I moved my blanket from one corner of the backyard to the next. The girls who were observing, began to giggle out loud. I peeked up from my book, when I heard the giggles and laughter. Apparently, I'd moved my blanket to all four corners of the yard, unaware of what I was doing.

I felt slightly embarrassed that my behavior was a bit peculiar, but I sensed an enormous struggle going on inside of me, and I hadn't a clue why I felt so restless and unsettled. Eventually, I went back to my room and tried to concentrate on my book. The struggle was even worse. Every minute that same request would play in my mind and I was becoming irritated. I knew my mother wasn't expecting me until the following week, but I felt so frustrated with this harassment that I finally gave into it. After packing a few clothes, I jumped a bus in Toronto, heading to Hamilton.

Knowing that my mother wasn't expecting me, I wondered if she'd be home. Beside the brick stone church was a small brick house where my mom and aunt lived. I knocked many times on the front door, then went to the back door and knocked many times there. No one answered, so I thought of finding a pay telephone to call one of my aunts to see if they knew where my mother might be. But instead of doing that, I noticed that one of the basement windows was opened ajar, and with a big push, I was able to open it wide enough to crawl through.

I glanced briefly across the property to the Seventy-day Adventist church and began to chuckle inside. Here I was trying to break into my mother's new house which was situated beside a church. All I needed was the police to find me breaking and entering. Wouldn't Mom be surprised if I was caught. I could see the newspaper headlines now, 'Elisabeth Newton charged with breaking and entering. She was only trying to visit her lonely mother residing beside a stone church.'

Once inside the unfamiliar home, I climbed down into something, but I wasn't sure what it was. It turned out to be an empty laundry tub. At least it wasn't full of water. I seemed to have twisted my ankle while trying to climb down. Once out of the laundry tub, I limped across the room, hoping to find a light switch. It was then I discovered some stairs going up to the next level. Slowly and deliberately, I ascended these and to my relief, found myself in a small kitchen. In the meantime my mother was on the third floor, listening to a religious broadcast on television. She hadn't heard anyone knocking on her door. However, I must have frightened her to death, because she reluctantly came down a flight of stairs, after hearing some noises in the basement. We were both startled, when we bumped into each other in the living room.

Once we got over the shock of seeing each other, Mom said she hadn't been expecting me until the following week. She asked me why I came earlier, but I didn't know what to say. I didn't even know myself why I'd suddenly changed my mind and appeared at her house.

After we talked for a while, I said goodnight to mom and went upstairs to bed. My tradition each night before sleeping was to turn on my cassette player and listen to some Spiritualist speak about the spirit world. As I was nicely settled in bed listening to one such speaker, there came a knock at my door. It was Mom, wanting me to meet someone downstairs who'd came for a visit. My radar antennas went up, because I knew that perhaps that 'someone' could be a leader of 'some' church she belonged to. He would probably invite me to come to church and learn the Bible. Reluctantly, I made my way downstairs, trembling inside.

Sure enough, Mom introduced me to Pastor Milliken, the minister of her church. I felt trapped and scared. But not wanting to appear rude we shook hands, and allowed him to open up the conversation. My plan was to listen graciously for awhile then dismiss myself quickly. However what happened next totally unnerved me.

He was wearing an ordinary suit, not a black suit with a white collar like a priest would wear. He was very pleasant to talk to, and surprisingly enough, he talked about everything but religion. A real conflict was battling inside of me. Without intending to ask this pastor any questions, I found myself blurting out, "What is truth?" I immediately regretted asking him this. However, he was delighted that I'd asked this important question, and commented, "I would be more than happy to answer your question, but first let me go to the car to get something." I insisted that I didn't want anything to do with the Bible, if that was what he was going for. He just told me to wait awhile, that he would be right back.

Mom made herself scarce all of a sudden and didn't return to the living room until the pastor came back with not only one Bible but two. My mind was racing like a animal struggling to get loose from a trap. I just sat there on the couch unable to move. The minister looked me straight in the eyes and told me how Christ had died for me and everyone in the world. He also told me how much He truly loves me, and the gospel news of salvation. He explained that Christ's magnificent gift of his grace was freely obtained, if we would ask Jesus for it. These words were totally foreign to me for in my past religious experience there was no hope of ever obtaining unconditional love from this man called Jesus. I then remarked to the minister, " This Christ doesn't accept everyone, especially as big a sinner as me, and that I had given up hope of ever receiving His love." The minister listened to me attentively then he quoted many Bible passages from God's Word, and I was very impressed with how he knew his Bible so well. He quoted many Bible texts on the love of Jesus, especially the text found in John 3:16. My conscience began to be at peace as my inward struggles were slowly dissolving.

Gradually, Pastor Milliken took me to the Old Testament Book of Daniel, explaining the prophecy of Daniel 2, all the way down to the end of time. It seemed the Holy Spirit had convicted me strongly, as I listened to a description of great events in world history leading right up to the times we are living in (the feet of iron and clay). It totally blew me away. For the very first time in my life I could see beyond the dark tunnel to the Light of the world. Until now, I could never be really sure what was worth holding onto. Finally I had something solid, a foundation to build on.

That moment is permanently etched in my mind as the most significant event of my life. My hardened heart, which hid my real feelings, broke at that precious moment as Christ came down and healed my broken heart replacing it with His. I finally ended my old journey of bondage, a life of slavery to a guru, and began my new spiritual journey, hand in hand with my new Master and Savior . The first love of Jesus can be ongoing and fresh everyday.

It is intriguing how the Lord allowed my path to cross with this special minister of God at the right moment. The minister explained to me later that he was on his way home from vacations when a strong impression came over him to visit my mother, as late as it was. His family had been waiting in the car. He believed it was the Holy Spirit impressing upon his heart to stop. It was exciting to see how God's plan was turned perfectly.

One look on my mother's face and I knew how happy she was to see her daughter accept Jesus as her personal Savior. She kept calling it a miracle of God. Tears of joy were being shed late that evening as we three celebrated God's unconditional love.

The Lord even knew what kind of minister would reach me spiritually. Mom must have spoken to the minister beforehand explaining to him how adamant I was against organized religion, because he never once invited me to church.

After my third Bible study with the pastor, I received an urgent telephone call from my sister in British Columbia, 3,000 miles away, pleading with me to come and stay with her. She'd had fallen ill and needed someone to be with her. Realizing that I was the only single sister left in our family, I felt it my duty to be with her. When I told the pastor of my plan, he was sympathetic about my sister's situation, but tried to persuade me to stay and continue my Bible studies a little longer before leaving. Even though I wanted to stay and continue the studies, my mind was made up to go.

Before I left by train, my mother along with the minister, had a prayer for God's protection and blessings upon me. He also gave me some Bible lessons to study while traveling on the train the next five days and said that he would contact Pastor Westrate in Chilliwack to prepare him to continue Bible studies with me.

Finally the train started moving along on the tracks, heading West. A young native Canadian man approached me and said he'd noticed I had a Bible. He was a Christian too, and wished to discuss the Bible with me. So I invited him to sit in the empty seat beside me. It seemed providential that God would send someone to me on the train to whom I could witness.

We discussed different Bible texts and since Dan was more familiar with God's word, I listened to what he had to say. Then he began to open up and tell me his life story and the tragedies he was suffering. He even disclosed information about his uncle killing two men in their family, and how his anger had brought him close to murdering a man himself. This guy had deserved it, he assured me. At that point I felt quite uncomfortable and sent a quick quiet prayer up to God, asking Him not to send someone so risqué to me the next time. After Dan finished his lengthy story, I suggested we study more of God's Word since I wanted to study the Bible lessons Pastor Milliken gave me. He consented, and we looked up different Bible texts that pertained to salvation, what happens to people after death and other Bible doctrines. Dan kept quite silent for quite awhile after our Bible study, and excused himself and left. It seemed obvious that the Holy Spirit was stirring his heart for he seemed disturbed by what he discovered in the Bible.

Once we arrived at the Chilliwack train station, my sister Susan spotted me and came towards me. We embraced with tears of joy in our eyes. It was the first time we'd met for almost ten years. Dan, the young man on the train came up , and I introduced him to my sister. He then asked if he could speak to me alone about something. A little hesitant, I reluctantly stepped aside to hear what he had to say. He proceeded to say that his reason for being here in British Columbia was to lead an Indian Pow Wow in front of Vancouver Parliament

Buildings. He wanted me to help him lead out with this. Since I was a Christian like him, he felt God would answer their prayers to pass the Indian Rights laws, on behalf of his people. I told him that I was not informed on these issues and that I doubted Christ would lead out in any Pow Wow if He was on earth. I said 'I am sorry but I must decline.' He appeared disappointed, but understood my concern.

My sister lived in a town called Sardis. When I got off the train in Chilliwack, I planned someday to return to the town to view its majestic mountains. As my new found faith in Jesus was growing, I wanted to share Him with my sister and her friends. They probably felt clubbed over the head with my preaching, and began making excuses to avoid hearing me talk about the Bible. As I look back on this event, I can only blush recalling how overzealous I was about sharing this new message from God's Book with everybody around me.

As time was passing on, Susan's health improved considerably. Even though she wanted to return home with me, she said something kept her there among the majestic mountains and the beauty of British Columbia. I was single and had no immediate desire to go home just yet. We decided to move not far away to a city called Chilliwack where I could find a job in an office somewhere. We found the ideal little house for us. It was a bungalow with three bedrooms, immaculately clean and modern. The owner, who lived next door, told us in his Russian accent that we could share his vegetable garden, which extended into our backyard. It was a cozy little city with high mountains protecting it from the outside world. If one looked straight up to the top of one of the mountains, from where we were living, a view of a sculptured polar bear could be clearly seen. It was breathtaking to see God's handiwork in the mountains and hillsides.

One day as I was walking around familiarizing myself with this new town, I came across a medium sized modern church, with brown brick siding. When I read the sign in the front of the church, my mouth fell open. I'd completely forgotten my promise to the minister back East, that I would look up his church here in Chilliwack, and pursue my Bible studies with the new pastor. I'd completely forgotten that the minister in Chilliwack was already awaiting my arrival. I'd spent close to three months outside Chilliwack, not even thinking of contacting any church minister. In fact, my plans were to worship on my own in the mountains and not bother with any church organization. Now I was at crossroads, and found myself struggling with the idea of whether it was worth going to any church. I really didn't see the importance and a strong urge to pass by entered my mind a few times.

It was Wednesday night and I noticed that there were a lot of cars in the parking lot. Suddenly a strong urge from within led me to go inside. Feeling very sheepish and cautious, I slowly opened up the door and peeked inside. An older lady noticed me and invited me in. It was too late to turn back. She wanted to know if I was visiting from somewhere else. I was invited to come in and join in the prayer meeting. It was all so foreign to me, not knowing what they were discussing, and not knowing anyone. The minister suddenly stopped what he was saying and glancing at me, asked me to stand up and introduce myself. I had to admit I felt very awkward, but I reluctantly got up and introduced myself. Then unexpectedly he asked me if I was the girl from Hamilton with whom he was suppose to have Bible Studies. When I hesitated, he said that Pastor Milliken had called him and told him about me. He also wanted to know what had taken me so long? At that point I felt awkward , and wanted to leave the church and never come back. However, I am glad I didn't. Later on I became accustomed to his sense of humor and strong hand shake. At that time, I wasn't familiar with different temperaments and how they affected others. But I know now that this minister had to be a high sanguine and an extrovert.

After prayer meeting, he approached me quickly, and arranged to meet with me for Bible studies. When he arrived at our home for the first time we studied different Bible doctrines. Over times, the studies were going well, but for some reason I didn't recall receiving a study on Satan, or Lucifer, and how deceptive he was. This study of Satan would have prepared me for what took placed next.

One time at church, while listening to a sermon by the pastor, I felt strong invisible hands around my throat, trying to choke me. I could hardly breathe. I started to gasp for air, slowly got out of my seat, and went outside to sit down. The choking feeling disappeared eventually, and this strong thought came to me, "Elisabeth, don't make yourself too comfortable in this church, because this is not the church God has in mind for you." Not recalling ever hearing about Lucifer or Satan, I thought it was a warning from God. Words could not express how confused and disappointed I was to hear those words. I finally went back into the church with a heavy and troubled heart sensing that I had to make a decision to leave soon. No one in the there knew about the struggles I was having.

Indeed, I was having many trials in several areas of my life, and couldn't understand why God would torment me like this. Strangely enough, I couldn't help but notice the contrast between my current life; how it seemed to be a battle field in comparison to my old life, when I was deeply involved in the New Age Movement. I'd felt so much at peace back then. I was beginning to have doubts about learning more about this church. Despite all these horrific struggles inside of me, though, I kept them tucked inside myself, never sharing these fears and doubts with anyone.

As our Bible studies were coming to a close, the minister asked me if I would like to be baptized, and I told him I'd have to pray about it first. Several weeks later the minister popped by, and nonchalantly handed me a Bible guide on Satan and his deceptive ways. He'd said he forgotten to give this lesson to me before and asked that I read it thoroughly. When I did so, I was dumbfounded and relieved at the same time. It was such a relief to know that God didn't want me out of His church after all, and that Lucifer was after my soul instead. From sheer thankfulness to God for making my crooked paths straight, I made plans for baptism.

Finally, one snowy evening in November, my sister gave birth to her son Joaquin. I was an aunt for the fourth time around, and enjoyed holding this precious little boy.

Each morning I'd wake up at 5 a.m. to pray and read the Bible for an hour, before doing my Hatha Yoga exercises for forty minutes. If I had time I'd eat on the run before going to work. My days and nights were full, but I had a real assurety in my heart now that I had found a purpose for living.

The date for my baptism was drawing close but my friend who was supposed to be baptized with me wasn't quite ready to make that commitment yet. I remember promising to wait for her. One day at church the minister's mother came up to me and asked when was I going to be baptized. I explained to her that I was waiting for my friend to be ready, so we could be baptized together. I'll never forget her words. She said, "What if she decides never to be baptized, and you are still waiting?" She quoted some texts which said that when the Holy Spirit moves one to be baptized, not to hesitate, for God is eagerly awaiting my decision. It didn't take me too long then to decide on the date of my baptism. I found out later that my friend did not get baptized after all. I felt reassured that this saintly Christian woman was used by God to help me make the right choice.

The night of my baptism was a time to rejoice for two reasons. Following Christ's example of baptism, of being immersed in water, symbolized His death and His resurrection to life. This new commitment I made in Christ held new meaning as a new Christian had my sins and guilt buried and I arose a new person in Jesus.. The other reason for my happiness was that I had no attacks or threats on my life from Satan. I felt so free, and no more in bondage.

The Lord also provided me with an office job at the British Columbia Conference office of the Seventh-day Adventist Church. I truly admired the president of the British Columbia Conference. He was a genuine Christian and friend. I never got tired of hearing him answer his office telephone with these words, "Here's How." His Christian name was Howard, but he shortened it to How. The Christian staff were quite helpful and caring. However, there were a few episodes that occurred that turned out to be humourous and worth remembering.

One day George Vandeman, the television speaker for *It Is Written,* came to visit our office. I was busy watering the plants when the president of the conference introduced me to him as a new baptized Christian. I have to confess that I did admire his TV Religious Broadcast and felt honored to meet him. Awkwardly I told him that I was lacking a green thumb to which he commented, "Well, I can tell by the way you had watered the plastic plants as well." After quickly checking sure enough that was what I did. At that point I thought if only the floor had opened up and swallowed me I wouldn't have to ever face him again.

After a month of working at the conference, a staff member suggested that I meet this single man he recommended. This man I was told, was a stable Christian Adventist and financially set. I quickly thanked the staff member and told him I wouldn't be interested in meeting anyone right now. However, as the devil planned it, I was introduced to this chap who consistently urged me to accept him as a prophet. He not only knew the Scriptures exceptionally well, but believed he could foretell the future. Apparently, we were part of the prophetic future, and he wasted no time in telling me that God revealed to him that we should marry. He decided that in the first two weeks after we'd met. I was quite shocked and wanted to get as far away from him as possible. However, through his persistence and my lack of knowing the will of God for my life, I began to weaken and was convinced that God wanted me to obey him by marrying this guy. But this fanatic really began to irritate me. He even cut out my wedding dress without consulting me. I thank God for sending me sincere close Christian friends like Gloria and Alfred Greaves who rallied around and warned me not to marry him. I found out that he'd been married before in Denmark. The rumor about his four marriages, broke the proverbial camel's back. I decided to break off my wedding plans with him and despite his compulsive obsession with his prophetic truth, he was no longer a part of my life. What freedom I felt.

Before ending this chapter I promised my two friends, Gloria and Alfred Greaves that I would share this funny story with my readers about what happened to us one weekend at their home . It took place at their house on a Friday night, a few weeks before my baptism. I had been invited to spend the weekend at their house. Alfred arrived home from work and he enthusiastically showed us a bottle of liquid cleaner to clean the small furnace situated in the living room. He quickly demonstrated how to use it by climbing a chair and pouring some of the liquid in the pipe of the furnace.

After supper we cleaned up and had worship. We enjoyed singing hymns, and after scripture reading and prayer we welcomed in the Sabbath. When it was time for bed we all said goodnight, and I made up my bed on the living room couch. It was early in the morning when I suddenly heard this sudden explosion coming from the furnace. I jumped so fast off the couch that my head felt dizzy. Soot flew all over the room landing on the window curtains, table cloth, floor and walls; not to mention the soot all over my face and hair.

Gloria and Alfred ran downstairs to witness the mess in the living room. Finally, all the family, and I ended up sleeping on mattresses in their bedroom. Morning came too soon as we reluctantly crawled from our mattresses to prepare for church.

Mother and James the oldest of the three who died in the fire

Mother with Nelson the second oldest of the three who died in the fire

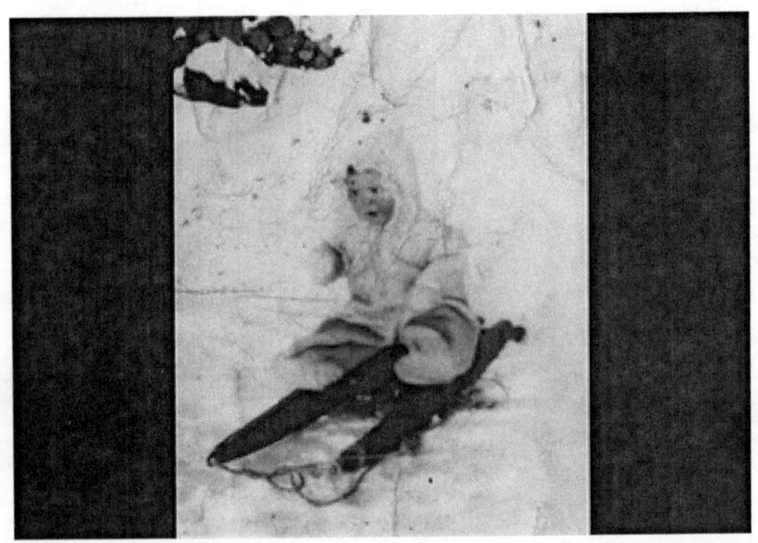

(Elisabeth I) nickname Betty-Anne, the third youngest who died.

Mother loved cross-country skiing

Mother with Sandra to the left, Elisabeth to the right, and Nadine in the center

Nadine and I are celebrating our First Communion. Pictured are Sandra, Susan, Nadine, Elisabeth, and Gregory

In the Park are Denise, Gregory, Susan, Nadine and in the back row, Elisabeth and Sandra

Celebrating our monthly dress-up and tea party

The Miss Canada Beauty Pageant 1967, taken in Niagara Falls, Ontario, Canada. Elisabeth is the fourth person on the right in the top row.

Richard and Elisabeth's wedding

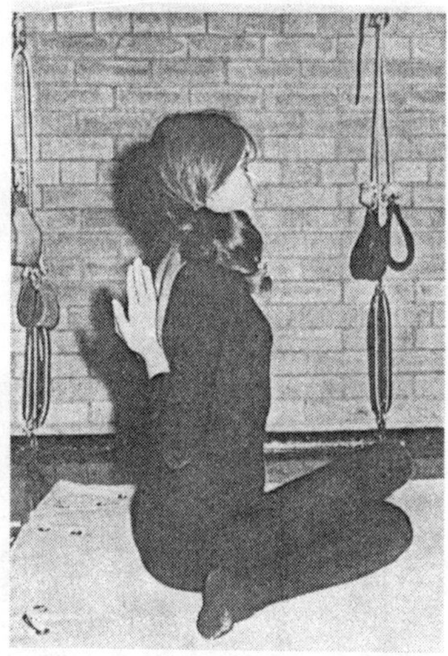

Elisabeth is practicing her Hatha Yoga Exercises at her work place.

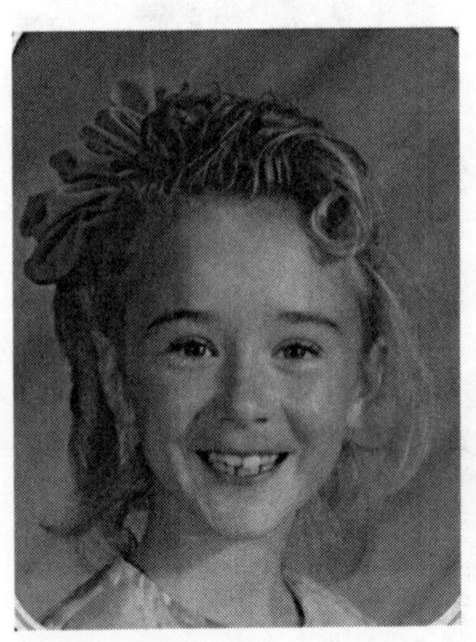

Rachelle age 7 (she sent this photo to Princess Diana and received a warm letter from her

Richard & Elisabeth in Burkina Faso, West Africa, wearing traditional costumes

The remains of our 84 Peugeot after the horrific accident in Burkina Faso, Africa

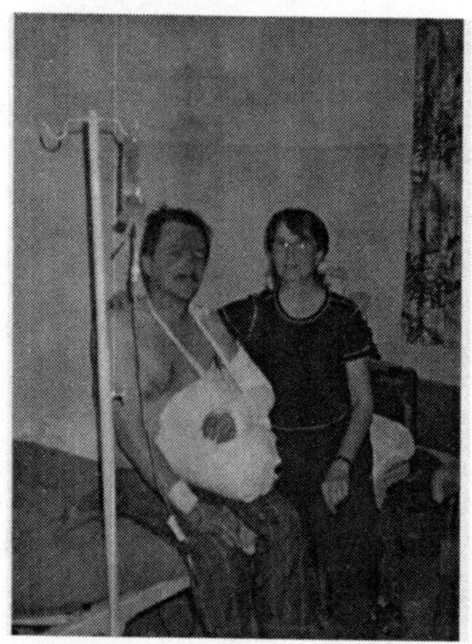

Richard on the mend in the maternity ward of the Burkina Faso hospital after accident

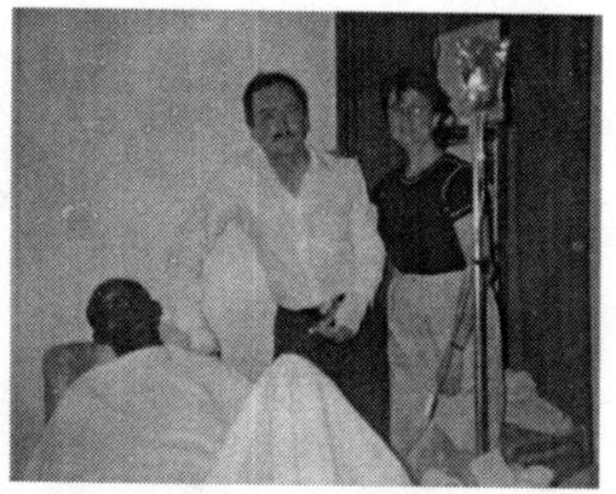

Visiting Michael, Richard's passenger, after his miraculous survival

Here we are in Kenya for Rachelle's graduation from Maxwell Adventist Academy

Elisabeth's graduation with her Bachelor of Theology degree. Richard was Dean of Theology at the University Adventist Zurcher in Madagascar

Elisabeth and Rachelle enjoying themselves at Calico, California

Mother is re-united with her three children in Matachewan, Ontario, Canada, where the fire took place.

"To reconcile man with man and not with God is to reconcile no one at all" by Thomas Merton

CHAPTER 14
RETURNING HOME

After a year in British Columbia, and working with other Christians, I felt I was prepared to return home and share the gospel news with my family and friends. A friend drove me to the train station with two large trunks loaded on the train heading East to Ontario. Since my family and relatives did not know Jesus like I did, I wanted to return home and witness to them. I had no idea at the time, just how much God was leading in this. The pleasant train ride exposed God's beauty even more, as the awesome mountains and vivid autumn colors of the maples and oak trees shouted for recognition. One evening, still traveling on the train, a sudden jerking crash woke me out of a sound sleep. Everyone bolted from their seats, half asleep to find out why the train had stopped so abruptly.

The news spread that the train had derailed, and that we all had to get out and take a bus to the airport. We wondered where we were. The derailment had happened in Saskatoon, Saskatchewan and since it would take a long time to repair, we were bused to the airport in Saskatoon and flown back to Vancouver, British Columbia, right where we started. There was a lot of confusion as to the whereabouts of our suitcases. One lady kept saying that she didn't care if she lost her clothes, as long as she could find her toothbrush. I thought the opposite. Finally we arrived at the Vancouver Airport with a guarantee that our suitcases would be with us. The sun was just rising when we were flown again to Saskatchewan. Looking like hound dogs with droopy bags under our eyes, we were bused once again to the train station, where we re-boarded the train going to Toronto. We were uncertain if our suitcases had made it on the train. I was concerned about my two trunks that were back in Saskatchewan. Once we had arrived in the Toronto train station, I was informed that my trunks would arrive in a few weeks. They kept their word.

As I was about to dismount from the train in Toronto, I noticed three people looking up at me: my mother, aunt, and Richard, a perfect stranger. He looked up at me for the first time with a big smile on his face. Of course their presence came as a complete surprise to me, because I'd made no arrangements to be picked up at the train station. I especially wondered why the stranger was here to pick me up. After many hugs and small talk, we drove back home to Hamilton.

Apparently, this young man Richard had been baptized in a Seventh-day Adventist church in Hamilton a week before my arrival. He'd taken Bible studies with the same minister with whom I previously had studied with in Hamilton. For many years while still living at home a desire to study the Bible had stirred within him. His parents were Roman Catholic and their church at that time, didn't allow the parishioners to read the Scriptures. Since he could not rest until he knew just what the Bible said on certain issues, he purchased a small home and moved out of his parents' house. He bought his first Bible that same week, and began to read it, but he knew that he needed to find someone to explain the Scriptures to him.

One day a Jehovah Witness knocked on his door and Richard was pleased to get some direction in answering his questions about the Bible. However, after a year of studies, he found that there were many issues that were still unclear. David, the Jehovah Witness who studied with him, said to Richard, "You have been studying with us for a year now and either you get baptised or we can't continue these studies. We can't waste our time with people who are not sincere." On the previous week, David told Richard about a Seventh-day Adventist lady who said, "We study the Bible too." So when he received this ultimatum, Richard said, "There are many questions that I raised that have not been clearly answered for me, so I can't be baptised when I don't believe such things, but last week you told me about a woman talking with your mother." He said, "Yes a Seventh-day Adventist." A few days later, Richard called the Seventh-day Adventist church and Pastor Milliken's wife answered. Richard explained that he would like to have Bible studies with the minister. Arrangements were made and Pastor Milliken began studying with Richard.

When the studies were almost over the pastor said, "You know Richard, I have never said this to anyone before, but I feel impressed to tell you that I believe some day you will become a minister just like me, and spread the gospel news wherever God leads you."

However, Richard quickly responded, "I don't think so, because I never had a calling from God to become a priest when I was attending the Catholic Church."

I was still standing at a crossroad in my life and didn't know what plans the Lord had in store for me now that I'd returned home. On top of that, the entire church, including the minister had a preoccupation with matchmaking Richard and I.

Pastor Milliken even told us that we should think of marriage. I tried to ignore his advice because I felt uncomfortable about marrying someone almost seven years younger than I.

About this time it seemed the Lord was leading me to be a Literature Evangelist. I'd be selling religiouis books door to door. I didn't have a car and it was difficult lifting heavy books onto the bus each day. It was a breeze greeting into the homes, but I was so fearful what I should say once I entered each home. Some how the Lord provided me the words, and my faith grew stronger from having to depend on God each day. I discovered that I was more successful selling the health books than the Bedtime stories and the others. Winter was fast approaching and it became more difficult walking door to door in the deep snow. I approached one door and knocked. After a long time a middle aged woman came to the door and even before I could give my little speech, she slammed the door on my face. I was taken aback as I stood there stunned. For some reason, unknown to me, I felt impressed to go to the backdoor and knock. The same lady came to the backdoor, and instead of slamming it she just laughed and said,. "You again. Since you are so persistent you must have something very important to sell. You might as well come in." The woman bought some health books and was very appreciative that I'd come.

"Success in marriage consists not only in finding the right mate, but also in being the right mate." by Eleanor Doan

CHAPTER 15

NEW AWAKENINGS

I had no idea that everyone in the church, including my mom and aunt, were busy praying and playing the role of matchmakers. They were eager to have Richard and I get married. One evening when Richard came to see me on my birthday, he asked me to close my eyes because he had a surprise for me. When my eyes were closed, he set a violin on my lap, and on one knee, he proposed to me. I honestly didn't know what to say. I muttered something about I'd have to think about it. I knew that Richard felt called to be a minister one day, my greatest fear was knowing that I would become a minister's wife. I felt that I couldn't measure up to these expectations. I thought I had to be perfect, and with musical talents. However, eight months before he was leaving for Canadian Union College I began to think of all the single girls he'd be meeting there at school, and right then and there I told him I'd marry him. The Lord helped me realize that Richard had some great attributes, and if I decided not to marry him, I would regret it for the rest of my life, despite my fears of having to be the perfect spouse of a pastor.

We announced our engagement in early December,1974, and everyone seemed so happy with our decision, especially my mom and aunt. However, something went terribly wrong shortly after our engagement that almost prevented us from getting married.. It happened on a Friday afternoon after I just returned from colporteuring. It was cold and windy outside, and I was relieved to be indoors where it was warm and comfortable. That evening, I started to feel awfully weak and dizzy. I decided to sleep on the chesterfield because I didn't think I could climb the stairs to my bedroom.

The next day Mom was getting ready for church, and when she came downstairs, she saw me lying on the chesterfield. I told her that I wasn't feeling very well. After checking my temperature which was quite high, she asked me if she should call the doctor, but I discouraged her from doing so. I reassured her that it wasn't that serious. So before she left the house, she told me she would look in on me between Sabbath School and church. It wasn't long after Mom left that I broke out in a sweat and my head started spinning around. I felt so hot, that all I could think of was turning the thermostat down. Gradually my body was completely paralyzed, except for my left hand. I couldn't even speak or utter a sound. When my mother returned she found me in a mute state and ran for a pad and pen so that I could write. I wrote words explaining that my body was paralyzed, including my mouth, and the only thing I could move was my left hand, my writing hand. She told me she would be back in a few minutes. While I awaited her return I knew down deep inside my heart that Satan had attacked me because he didn't want me to marry a minister. He knew that if I followed through on this decision, he would lose me as one of his victims. I heard some voices at the door, and there stood

Mom, Richard, and a Bible worker, Gloria, and her husband Paul Lawson, along with a few other members of the church. They looked at me with concern and said they would audibly pray for God to intervene and heal me. Then there was some discussion about taking me to the local hospital. In my mind I wanted to go to Dr. Buxton, a Christian woman doctor in Toronto, an hour away from Hamilton. When I gestured to Richard that I need the pad and pen, I wrote that I didn't want to go to the local hospital, but instead to see Dr. Buxton at the Branson Adventist Hospital in Toronto. Finally, they decided that Paul and Gloria (members of the church), would drive me there, and Richard would follow us in his car. When I looked up briefly at Richard's face, he looked fearful and there were tears flowing down his cheeks.

It was difficult to breathe as the pressure on my chest grew worse. I was carried out and placed horizontally in the back seat of the car, since I couldn't sit up or bend. In my mind I was going to die and there was nothing anyone could do about it. I was familiar with Satan's attacks from time to time, and I couldn't see myself living much longer. Of course, I was saddened to know that the plans for our wedding would be cancelled. We arrived an hour later at Dr. Buxton's home, picked her up, and headed to the hospital. She climbed into the front seat of the car, and turned around to face me. She then took my hand to pray for a healing from God. Almost immediately the pressure on my chest left and my body was no longer paralyzed. What a surprise to find that I could actually move again and talk. The others were relieved and happy to see that I could sit up and walk into the hospital with minimal assistance. The doctor ran tests on my esophagus since I had been complaining about throat problems, and indigestion.

The tests revealed that I had a stomach hernia due to lifting heavy books, along with lack of sleep. My literature evangelist days were over for now, since I couldn't carry any more heavy books. Dr. Buxton said there was so much pressure on my chest, and I felt so weak and dizzy because of the stomach hernia that was causing a lot of pain. However, I decided not to share the real reason for my illness, because I didn't want any more attacks from Satan.

"Marriage begins when you sink in his arms and ends with your arms in the sink." by Eleanor Doan

CHAPTER 16
TYING THE KNOT

Several years prior to meeting Richard and making plans to wed him, my friends and I were playing with an Ouija Board. I was prompted to ask it whom I would marry and when? The object kept moving to the initials 'rp' whom I didn't know. Then it was asked when would I marry? This time the object moved from May 21, to April 6 several times. I stored this information, and recalled it later when I had made plans to marry. This experience revealed to me that Satan can perform these small miracles to try to convince some people that he knows their destiny. As a Bible believer I would sooner let God direct my destiny.

We finalized our plans and wedding date with Pastor Milliken for the long weekend in May, 1975. In March, a young new couple attending our church decided they wanted to marry on that date. We decided to change our plans and marry a month earlier. Lacking assertiveness to stand on my decision, I changed our wedding date to April 6.

We will never forget that day. The weather brought the worst snow storm in fifty years and many of our relatives from Quebec and Northern Ontario couldn't make it. No photos could be taken outside, but we at least had pictures taken inside the church.

Four months after our marriage, we wished for a sign from God to know if Richard should go into the ministry and attend Canadian Union College, the name of the Adventist College back then. We would need to have our little cottage on the river sold within two weeks before we planned to leave for Alberta. Two weeks to the day our little cottage sold and we left for Alberta.

The first Friday of our arrival at Canadian Union College we were invited to join a group of students after church for a picnic and mountain climbing. After the picnic we started our climb down a mountain when a student couple were coming up. We were introduced to a theology student and he was just about to introduce me to his wife when I opened up my mouth and asked him if that woman beside him was his mother. It's a good thing that they were a matured Christian couple were able to laugh at themselves, because they told me a surprising thing that the woman was "his wife and not "his mother." It seems I was getting very good at putting my foot in my mouth... how I wished that the mountain would swallow me up and I could disappear. Despite this incident, we became very close friends.

We rented a small basement apartment with no furniture except a borrowed mattress and a table and chairs. We also noticed that we didn't live alone...there were several cheeky greyish mice with pretty pink ears that enjoyed sharing our staples.

On our first morning of school we were up very early making toast. As I was waiting for the toast to pop, I was leaning against the table yawning away when suddently a mouse popped from the toaster with his tail on fire. The mouse was screeching so loud and running so fast from the table, that in my frenzied state of mind, I was doing the same as him, running in the same direction as the mouse. Finally, Richard came up behind me with a puzzled look on his face asking me over and over again what the problem was. I decided to go back to bed to recuperate from that adventure. After awhile I got used to having company while we ate and slept. I stopped doing my dancing rituals everytime we saw a cheeky pink ear greyish mouse.

We experienced some interesting challenges as new Christians, which eventually molded and shaped us for God's ministry. One of the challenges was that we couldn't find immediate employment at school and we were left with hardly any money.

Financial struggles were pressing in on Richard and me, since we couldn't find full time employment. We were down to our last bit of food one Christmas and very hungry. A remarkable experience turned us around though, when out of the blue, a Christian friend from back East, sent us a cheque for $50.00. He had no idea what financial struggles we were having, because we had never kept in touch with him after we'd moved to Canadian Union College. We were amazed and grateful to God, and to our distant friend for providing us with some groceries for a nice Christmas dinner. Right after the New Year, we both found full time jobs, and didn't worry about finances for a while.

My new job was at the Roland Michener Recreation Center working in the office as a secretary and receptionist. There were 1500 physically and mentally challenged residents who lived on the property. Where I worked at the recreation centre many of the residents would enter the building daily to go to the swimming pool or do other remedial activities with the recreational therapists. One day my boss, Igor Lozinski, had a board meeting planned with the staff across the hall from where my office was. When everyone asrrived and settled into their chairs, I heard this loud voice belonging to my boss. Apparently, Bobbie, who was a resident, often loved stealing light bulbs from light fixtures and eating them. Since the light bulb was missing in the board room Igor couldn't turn on the light.

Another time, while working at the same place, one of the residents came running up to me as I was walking across the hall, and gave me the biggest bear-hug that I ever could imagine. Finally, when I was let go, and the wind was knocked out of me, I easily fell to the ground groaning. After that experience I'd run in the opposite direction when I saw that particular resident. When we left school and work we were sad to leave both places. We were learning how to become new disciples for Christ with what we were learning at school and practising these Bible principles our workplace.

Being a recent Christian in the school was a bigger adjustment for me than for Richard. There seemed to be different levels of Christianity on campus, and I wasn't sure where I fit in. The school offered an environment of protection and yet I felt isolated from the real world. After four years living at Canadian Union University, we were ready to face real life situations working in the ministry of a church.

Richard gave me wise counsel when he reminded me that living in a school environment is not the same as living in a church setting where what was learned at school can be put into practice.

One morning in July as I entered our apartment after church the telphone rang and the call was from my sister back East in Canada. Apparently, my stepfather died of a sudden heart attack. Very disappointed and in a shock I thought to myself, "This can't be possible Lord. I had plans to go home this summer and let him know that I had forgiven him for some of the physical and verbal abuse he'd vented on me while growing up. And now it's too late." After a lot of anguished prayers and tears, I accepted the fact that even though it was too late to speak to my stepfather about Jesus, I had to learn to let the past go, and live for the present and future. And since I had been able to forgive him, a real sense of peace and comfort flowed through my heart. I thanked the Lord for taking this heavy burden I carried around with me for most of my adult life. In Matthew 28:29, 30, it speaks about our burden being lifted by Jesus.

About six months before leaving the college, a funny thing happened. Three married couples decided to drive to the big city of Edmonton about ninety kilometers away from the school to celebrate birthdays. at the popular Spaghetti Factory Restaurant.

Since our old van didn't have any back seats, we put six lawn chairs inside, and we gingerly sat down. Whenever Richard turned a corner, our lawn chairs would sway sideways like weeping willow branches. At times the lawn chairs collapsed in the middle, with bodies in them. They say a picture is worth a thousand words. Well, this encounter could have landed us in the funniest videos, if only we would have brought a video camera with us.What a relief when we arrived at the restaurant to sit in real sturdy chairs that didn't collapse.

Inside the partially lit restaurant, we found a table in a far corner. Mary was proud of the new suit she bought her husband Jack Friesen. The suit was a pale blue summer suit. He looked handsome in it. He took great care not to soil it. When the energetic, free spirited waiter arrived at our table, we ordered immediately, because we hadn't eaten all day. When he returned with our food he was swaying back and forth, to the loud background music. He carried a large tray of dishes, balanced on one hand suspended high in the air. Suddenly, the salad dressing slipped off the tray and splattered all over our friend's new pale blue suit. Everyone immediately stopped talking, and fixed our eyes on our friend Jack. Despite the shocked look on Jack's face, we just couldn't keep from laughing. The waiter tried to apologize in his clumsy way, but it didn't take the stains off Jack's suit. Finally our food came and we all enjoyed it, despite the mishap. When we finished our meal, we were looking forward to our lawn chair ride home again.

One Sunday afternoon in March when the snow was melting, my girlfriend Glenna and I were walking down the campus road, gabbing away like two chipmunks. It was a lovely sunny day in spring, when the air smells fresh and the birds are busy making their nests. My girlfriend's husband, Rod and Richard were out together, driving down the campus road. At one point they saw us walking and stopped to ask when supper would be ready. That snapped us out of our spring mood. The last thing we wanted to do was to cook food when we were enjoying the beautiful balmy weather. They said they were inviting some visitors for supper, but wouldn't tell us who these visitors were. Before we could ask any more questions, they took off. We were left wondering.

We were at our mobile home preparing supper, when our husbands quickly came into the driveway. They jumped out of Rod's vehicle and into Richard's van and off they sped. Now we really became suspicious. But we decided to be obedient wives and wait the game out. We were cooking up a storm, when our fellows rushed into the house, and immediately shut all the curtains and told us they would be back in twenty minutes.

Finally, a half hour later, we heard the van pull into the driveway once again. We quickly looked out the window and there sitting in the back of the van were Bonnie and Jim, dressed in their all weather-coats, collars up and Al Capone hats on their heads. They looked like the actual Bonnie and Clyde of the movie screen. The van door opened and they peaked out cautiously, looking both ways before disembarking. One was carrying a movie projector. As I opened up the side door of our house, not sure if I should look both ways as well, they both raced into the kitchen. Noticing my puzzled look, they finally explained their reasons for this mysterious appearance.

Apparently the college committee of which they were a part had agreed to show the film "King of Kings" for the student body. Invitations had gone to the local area around the college, as well as far as two hours away, inviting people to come and see this film. In the meantime, one of the committee members decided that the movie was questionable and encouraged the committee to cancel the showing. You can imagine the scramble for Bonnie, Jim and other students having to make long distance telephone calls at the last minute to cancel the film. A few people were determined to see the movie, however, before it was sent back the next day. The rest of the story is obvious--place of movie--our house trailer. The curtains were already shut tight, lights were off, and we all ate our supper in the dark. This mystery was finally solved.

Two months before Richard graduated, a call came from our conference in Ontario, Canada. They needed a French pastor to minister to a two church district, one church in the area of Hawkesbury, situated at the border of Quebec on the Ontario side, and the other in Ottawa.

Before my husband started his new position as pastor, we took a month off and traveled to Europe. We traveled by Euro Rail through many countries in Europe and the British Isles, not knowing that two years later we would be returning to live in France.

We spent five gorgeous days on the island of Crete in Greece, swimming in the Mediterranean Sea and soaking up the sunshine. On our return trip from Greece, we were once again traveling on the train through Italy. We decided to stop overnight in Florence. It was early afternoon when we arrived in the beautiful artist belt of Italy, where a large sculpture of Michaelangelo stands in the center square of Florence. We traveled with backpacks everywhere and our loads were getting heavy from walking through the streets, trying to find a room where we could sleep. We had to walk single file, because the streets were so narrow.

Richard was leading the way and didn't know that I had fallen behind some distance. We'd been walking for about an hour and were still looking for a place to sleep. Suddenly, I noticed a small gentleman dressed up in a suit, walking close behind me. I thought I felt a hand reach up into my backpack and yelled to Richard to get his attention, but he was not within earshot. As I tried to walk a little faster, I noticed there was extra weight on my back. Since I didn't speak Italian, I said in French, "leave my backpack alone." Sensing that this person wasn't taking me seriously, I reluctantly turned around to face him. There stood the short man of about sixty, with a nice suit on. He started screaming Italian words at me, and I was trying to be heard and understood. I stood there completely helpless, while he extended his hand to show me his button had come off his suit. He then pointed at my backpack. Looking at his suit, it finally dawned on me that the buckle from the backpack had caught onto his new suit, and yanked off one of the buttons. It also dawned on me, that the extra weight on my back was probably due to him trying to pry his button loose from my buckle. My face turned slightly red, as I turned away saying under my breath in English, "It deserves you right for getting too close to my backpack, anyway."

It was a sunny day when we arrived in Brittany, on the west side of France, a small fishing port where the tides would leave the shore for long periods of time, and return later in the day to the harbor. Since we couldn't find a room to rent, we waited for the next train to take us from Brittany to another country. We had six hours to wait, so we walked around the little village and did some exploring. We noticed at one end of a park some of the older gentlemen playing a game called "Ball". It was a competitive sport and became very intense. After watching the game for quite awhile, we decided to take a walk through the forest, where we eventually lay down to relax on the dark green grass and fell asleep. We woke up with the sun filtering through the trees and children staring down into our faces and whispering among themselves. As soon as we got up and began speaking to them they quickly took off through the forest.

Finally our train came and we were on our way once again. We seemed to have spent half of our time traveling on the train, as we went from one country to another. Our vacation was coming to the end as we flew from Paris to Toronto Airport. Upon our arrival there, we were looking forward to a long, overdue sleep in our comfortable bed, but instead an unexpected surprise came our way.

"A woman is like a tea bag; you never know how strong she is until she gets into hot water." (A Wall Plaque)

CHAPTER 17

A PASTOR'S WIFE

Following a short stay with our family in Hamilton, we drove a rented moving van to Quebec to retrieve our furniture that was being stored in an old farmhouse. We arrived late at night. The place was way out in the country far from any main roads, and as we pulled up to the house we remembered that there were no lights, only the moon and the stars. We attempted to move things using only a flashlight. After great effort, we finally succeeded in getting some of our furniture onto the truck, including an old upright piano.

We ended up sleeping in the old farmhouse, despite my eagerness to leave as soon as possible. The place reminded me of the TV series called "Green Acres", minus the telephone on the telephone poll. The next morning we arose, as soon as the sun came up, and loaded the rest of our furniture.

I wouldn't recommend a move like that to anybody. I ended up going to the chiropractor for almost two months with back problems. It was a lesson well learned, at least until the next time.

As I previously mentioned, when we had lived in a school environment, my doubts about my Christianity were greatly tested and especially my doubts of being a successful pastor's wife. Richard's sound advice was to wait and see how big a difference we would notice from where we were to where God was sending us. He believed that ministering to a church would be rewarding and fulfilling. Our ministry in our first church proved Richard right in saying how happy and accepting the members would be. It didn't take long before I felt part of the church. After that, my passion for the ministry took off, because I felt I finally fit into my new surroundings.

Our years in Hawkesbury and Ottawa were rewarding years, as we made endearing friendships with these sincere new committed Christians like ourselves. This experience helped me to gain confidence as we moved from church to church.

Not long after we'd settled down in our nice large home, I had a miscarriage. That saddened us for awhile. We were anticipating having children after we left school. But life doesn't always turn out the way we plan. After two years in this church district, we were encouraged by Elder Samuel Monnier, World Mission Leader from the General Conference, to attend the Adventist school in Collonges, France, for a school year. Since Richard eventually had to complete his Master's of Divinity degree, he was able to take the first part of the Master of Arts degree at Collonges, France, for a year, then transfer all his credits to Andrews University and complete his Master of Divinity.

My mother spoke fluent French and wanted to see Europe, so she came to live with us during our school year in France. Mom and I joined different French classes to learn how to speak it European style. Since I wanted to learn the flute, I also took some flute lessons. My instructor was a student who knew only French, and at times when we ran into difficulty understanding each other, Richard or my mother would come to the rescue.

It was so great to explore different countries in Europe. The countries are so close to each other that it made traveling easy. On frequent breaks from school, we would drive our student friends, who didn't own a car, back to their home countries, where we were invited to stay with their families. This way we enjoyed Paris, France, Austria, and Italy.

Since the college was situated near the border of Switzerland we sometimes took advantage of the mild weather, and walked the six kilometers into Geneva. At the border crossing we had to show our passports to the guard, then we would hop a trolley to the shopping place in Geneva. Geneva is a city of contrasts, with historical places, and statues of religious reformers such as John Calvin, Martin Luther, and others at the University of Geneva. Not far from the Reformation Wall, John Calvin's church stands tall and majestic. The outside structure is gothic-looking and well preserved, even though it was built several centuries ago. Frequently, we would sit on the benches at the Reformation Wall facing the gigantic chiseled shaped figures and try to imagine what it must have been like to live in the 1500's.

One day, after school, my mother, Richard and I were visiting the University of Geneva and the Reformation Wall, when Richard decided to browse in one of the old used book stores, a favorite pastime of his. In the meantime, Mom and I decided to browse in some stores not far away. In one of the chocolate shops we couldn't resist buying a fourteen inch Suisse chocolate bar, intending to split it three ways. We returned to the bench at the wall, and we, unintentionally, ate most of the chocolate bar. It was so tasty, and there was only a small piece left for Richard. Well, when Richard returned and noticed the guilty looks on our faces, we confessed to our gluttony, and gladly gave him the rest of the chocolate. A day later Mom and I were so sick with stomach cramps that we were bed ridden while Richard took care of us.

Halfway through my French studies at the college, I became ill, and went to the hospital for a check up. The ultrasound showed a tubal pregnancy, and the doctor said that I must be operated on, as soon as possible. But the hospital was short of beds, and couldn't take me right away. I was sent back home, with only a faint hope that a bed would soon be free. My fear about the possibility of ever becoming a mother began to plague me, and I found myself grieving more and more. Finally, a bed was available, and I went to the hospital near Collonges. Two Italian doctors operated on me for three hours. They told me that they had encouraging news for me. The doctors believed that within a year, I'd have a good chance of a healthy pregnancy. My heart wanted to believe them, but I didn't allow myself to get my hopes high. After our school year was over, we flew home to Canada for only four days to visit our families, and then drove straight to Andrew's University in Berrien Springs, Michigan.

Richard enrolled in the Master of Divinity Program. Summer was changing rapidly into the autumn season, and the winds were blowing the vivid colored leaves off the trees and unto the campus. A month after school began, a nice couple needed someone to care for their two small boys. When the couple found out that we, the Parents, were parentless, they encouraged us to care for their boys, saying, "the last lady who cared for them was also wanting a baby and did get pregnant". They told us it could be contagious. Of course, I didn't take the comment seriously, but I enjoyed minding the small boys during the day for a few hours, since it took my mind off my loss.

The winter cold began to settle in by November. As I tried to struggle out of bed one morning, feeling very nauseated, I dragged myself to the washroom and began vomiting. After daily occurrences of the same sickness, it dawned on me that I must be pregnant. But fear struck me as I struggled with the thought of an unhealthy pregnancy. When I was three months along, I told Richard not to say a word to anyone about it. However, Richard was too excited not to share the good news with everyone he knew.

I lost twenty-nine pounds during my first five months of pregnancy, so the doctor decided to put me on a WIC program until I was full term. This nutritionist program were used for pregnant women who had high risk problems. This entailed the Nutritionist signing me up for food coupons.

A surprised baby shower was planned by Richard and another friend. Since my girlfriend, Sonia, was also pregnant and due a month after me, a surprised double shower was planned. We had a wonderful time opening up baby gifts, chatting with our friends, and eating too much.

A few weeks later, a horrific tornado hit Berrien Springs, and Richard and I went out to look at the sky. We noticed dancing clouds swirling around the sky, and there was an old oak tree that broke in half. I ran back to the house and opened the door quickly. Richard was behind me but the wind pushed him away from the house. I began panicking and yelled out to him, "Hang on to my hand I don't want to be a widow while expecting a baby." What a relief when he grabbed my hand tightly and I pulled him in the door.

One Friday night there was a special communion service at Andrews campus church and the married couples were invited to attend. A light supper was served, followed by a foot-washing service. After eating a small portion of food, we were invited to go to a separate room delegated for married couples to wash one another's feet. What a disaster that turned out to be. I no sooner bent down to wash Richard's feet in the basin, when all I could think of was vomiting. I managed to restrain myself and quickly ran to the washroom.

In the meantime, Richard noticed all the couples around him were finished and leaving the room, as he waited for what seemed like an eternity for me to return. Finally I came back and noticed that his feet were still in the basin. He was encouraged to dry his feet quickly, put on his socks and shoes and take me home. So much for enjoying my first months of pregnancy.

All the bouts of sickness proved worthwhile later when I delivered a healthy baby girl. She arrived at 7 a.m. on a Wednesday, Sept. 1, 1983 in the hospital at Hamilton, Ontario, Canada. Finally my deep desire was fulfilled--that of being a mother.

Following Richard's graduation, he was called to be the associate pastor of a large church in Toronto. After our frequent moves the past few years, we were glad to settle in one place for at least another nine months. We looked forward to finally unpacking our belongings and forgotten treasurers that had been stored away for almost four years. Despite the January freeze, we looked forward to setting up house.

After nine months of internship in Toronto, we were transferred to a two-church district, three hours apart in northern Ontario. The area where we lived had a population of 5,000 and was predominately French. It was an isolated spot with the small memberships of our churches scattered far and wide. I thought we'd reached the end of the earth when we arrived in Haileybury. To think that I was born even further north in Matachewan, a place we left when I was three years of age! I found the isolation difficult at times, and didn't know how I'd cope without my friends around me. There was only one

Adventist lady who lived 3 kilometers from us, but she was hardly available. We lived in a predominantly French Catholic community and we had to learn a different approach to making friends. Despite the isolation we felt, gradually life in the north became tolerable. After some bouts of depression, and post-natal blues, things picked up when I joined a community choir in New Liskeard, eight kilometers away. This choir was made up of some thirty-five to forty persons from various religious and ethnic backgrounds. We enjoyed great social times together. I made some good friends from this community choir, and some of us still keep in touch. There were a lot of socials planned for the choir members which made it well worth attending.

We have photos to prove Richard was not only a fisher of men, but a fisher of fish. Sometimes between Bible studies, he would bring our two-year-old daughter, Rachelle, fishing. We have a photo of Rachelle holding the fishing rod with a large sturgeon it, that stood taller than she was. From that time forward, she was addicted to fishing, just like her father.

I worked part-time in the office at the Children's Aid Society. There were a lot of abusive cases of children, that wrenched my heart. However, it was a growing experience for me. I had to leave these burdens at the feet of Christ because He alone could help them. Many times I would pray for God's direction and wisdom on how to transmit Christ's love to these unfortunate victims. I would find comfort in the Bible, especially from Matthew 11:28-30.

We have fond memories of our northern churches and appreciated the members dedication. There was one comical experience that stands out in my mind. A youth group from Richmond Hill, near Toronto, planned to come to our church district to put on a weekend program. They were to arrive at the church Friday, before supper, with air mattresses, sleeping bags and food. The event was being organized by four adults who would stay with them in our small church, and help with the Sabbath program.

Some church friends who planned to stay at our house arrived early for the weekend. That Friday evening, we commented on how smoothly things must be going at the church, since we hadn't heard any news from the group so far that day. During our supper hour there had been no emergency phone call, and we seemed pretty relaxed and confident that everything was under control. However, just as we were ready to retire about 11 p.m. the phone rang, and a young man at the church wanted to know how to shut off the water in the baptistery. Apparently water was overflowing, and flooding the basement and it was seeping into some of the rooms where the youth were sleeping. The caller commented that some of his clothes were even floating down the basement hall.

On that urgent note, Richard and Raffy grabbed pails, rags, and mops, and ran out the door. Knowing they would be quite some time before returning, I decided to dash into bed and get some sleep, as baby Rachelle, then a year old, awoke early in the morning.

Just as I was about to snuggle under the warm covers, I heard Rachelle crying from her bedroom. Not accustomed to hearing her cry at night, I quickly climbed out of bed, wondering what was the matter. I no sooner turned on her bedroom light, than I quickly sized up the problem. She was standing up in her crib, crying and clutching her doll, which was covered with vomit, along with the soiled sheets and blankets. Even her hair and pyjamas were covered with it. Knowing that my work was cut out tout de suite, I brought her downstairs, with her doll, sheets and blankets, and ran some warm water in the tub. After a good scrub, clean pyjamas, and some children's Tylenol to take down her fever, she seemed to want to sleep.

By then it was around midnight. I settled her down once again with clean sheets and blankets. Then I rinsed the bed clothes, doll and pyjamas, and quickly ran to bed for the second time, hoping for some needed sleep. Before long, Rachelle started to cry again. This time I bolted out of bed and turned on her bedroom light, only to face the exact scenario and go through the same procedure as before. I felt thankful that she didn't get sick like this very often. Just as I was about to rinse off more clothes and pyjamas, the fellows returned home with two garbage bags full of wet clothes. Apparently the young people's clothes were wet from the baptistery overflow, and they needed them dried by eight a.m. the next morning for the church program. I watched my beauty sleep slip away, as I stood near the dryer waiting for the clothes to dry. Needless to say, I didn't see bed until four a.m. and then not for long. I felt like a dishrag, as I climbed out of bed at seven to check on how Rachelle was doing.

Later, when I arrived at the church, the lawn was fully decorated with wet clothes, and carpets. Boxes of clothes for charity had unfortunately been stored in the basement. As I stood there in front of the church, eyeing all the boxes and other things, a lady walking down the street stopped and asked, "Could you tell me what time the yard sale will be?" At first I didn't know what she was referring to, until she pointed to all the stuff in the yard. I was taken off guard and muttered something about, tomorrow being a better day to come and browse. It took me awhile to see the humor of that day.

As mentioned, we had a two church district in northern Ontario, one in Haileybury, the other in Timmins. But due to the great needs in Val D'or, Quebec, three hours away, my husband raised up a church company. It involved several Bible studies and baptisms. The Lord blessed this group in a remarkable way. It was a known fact that we spent more time in our car driving to these three churches than in our home. More important though were the precious souls that were won to Jesus, despite the distance of the churches. Before leaving this district, we could praise God for the fruitful ministry He planted there.

Guess what? We were on the move again. This time to Sudbury and the North Shore district. A few days prior to the move, Rachelle and I went to visit my mother in Cambridge. We'd planned to return home to help with the move, but Rachelle came down with an infected spleen, and had to stay put for one week at my mother's. After several days of antibiotics she did recuperate. Finally moving day arrived at our home in Sudbury, and the church conference truck showed up while Richard was in town. Unfortunately, our car transmission had burned out, leaving Richard with thirty minutes to shop around for another used car. Then he raced home to load up the moving truck.

When Richard came to pick us up at Mom's, there was a used smaller car in the driveway. With a surprise look on my face I asked,"Where is our Nissan car, Richard?"

He said reluctantly, "The car transmission blew and I had thirty minutes to buy another car before the conference moving truck came."

I was so disappointed that our car was gone, and that we wouldn't be driving it any longer. But I spoke up quickly, and said, "Well, can we call the person who bought our Nissan for parts, and ask him to repair it, because we really prefer it to this small clunker."

On our way to Sudbury, we stopped at a telephone booth to call the mechanic, and I prayed to God that somehow by a miracle, we would get our previous car back. The mechanic informed Richard that our car was at the auction, and it was too late to reclaim it. I was dismayed to hear the news, that our wonderful Nissan was in an auction already. Then a quiet voice seemed to say to me, "Elisabeth, even if the car transmission was fixed, the car had other problems, and eventually all of you could end up in a terrible car crash." I was so relieved to hear God's warning I shared this impression with Richard, and never questioned God again about our Nissan.

Richard had a large metal machine lathe weighing a ton, 2,000 pounds, to be moved on the truck It was cumbersome to move, so Richard made four metal wheels and sealed them to the bottom of the lathe, enabling it to roll up the ramp into the truck. It looked like the Grecian Trojon horse. Richard cautioned the mover to secure the ramp against the cement pavement of the garage so that the lathe wouldn't slip when it was rolled up. Unfortunately, the instructions were not carried through, and the mover fell between the planks and hurt his right knee badly. His assistant drove the truck to Sudbury, and after unloading our things, they drove to the nearest hospital to have his knee x-rayed. We were relieved to know that it was just a terrible sprain, not a fractured knee.

Our next two new churches situated in Sudbury and North Shore were three hours apart. With faith, we purchased a house in Val Thérèse near Sudbury, even though our previous house hadn't sold as yet. So we were faced with paying mortgages on two houses at the same time, and that was risky for us. Since the conference wanted us to be in the district before August we moved a month ahead of our furniture, and brought only our essentials with us to set up house. These consisted of our air mattresses, sleeping bags, a cottage refrigerator, a two burner camping stove, a lot of paper plates, cups, plastic cutlery, T.V., clothes and our Bibles.

The next morning after our arrival, the phone rang around 6:15 a.m. The bedroom telephone was already on the floor, so I didn't have far to reach from where we slept on the air mattress. An unfamiliar voice was on the other end of the phone. The woman was panicking because her daughter and son had lice and she didn't know what to do about it. Assuming the woman know where the pharmacy was, I advised her to look one up and call her closes pharmacist. There was a long pause on the other end, then quietly she asked, "Aren't you the new minister's wife that just moved in?"

"Yes", I said "and to whom am I speaking to? "I am a member of your church". She proceeded to tell me how worried she was that she and her children had lice, and her girlfriend from Southern Ontario was coming to visit her with her two teenagers. If her girlfriend found out that her children had lice, she wouldn't want to visit. I hadn't met either of these ladies, but felt that I would soon enough. The caller asked if her girlfriend and her two children could stay with us while she tried to get rid of the lice. It was my turn to comment. I glanced down at our air mattress. Finally I tried to describe the condition of our indoor camping facilities and our lack of furniture. Before the lady hung up, she asked if she could send up a short prayer to God, on our behalf, since we were in greater need than her family.

Since my husband is bilingual, he speaks French and English, the Conference felt this district would be a good match. Many of the church members were bilingual and Richard was to be the French speaker for the religious Revelation series on TV.

After settling into our new districts we felt at home with our churches, and we were glad to hear that there was an elementary church school for Rachelle. At times, Richard would teach conversational French to the church school students, and at one of these sessions, he set-up a restaurant scenario with the children participating in the skit. One student was the owner of a restaurant, a few students were waitresses, and the others were patrons who came to eat. The menu was in French, so when they ordered their food from the menu they had to speak French. Conversational French was good practice for them, and they seemed to enjoy the "hands-on"experience.

I became involved with the Pathfinder Club, as was our daughter Rachelle. We shared some wonderful times together with the Pathfinders on camping trips and camporees. I will always cherish these experiences. I'll never forget the many close friends we made in our different churches. We still keep in touch with them to this day. The one hardship that is inflicted on most pastor's families, is having to move so often. During our twenty-seven years in the ministry, most of the time we moved every two years. There were only two districts where we spent four years.

When the moving truck showed up once again, it was time to move on to Cornwall and Brockville Districts where we spent three years. At least in our Heavenly home, there will be no moving truck. These districts had challenges, like any other. In Cornwall the church membership was around forty-four. They had a passion and commitment to reaching the community through cooking schools, weight loss seminars, Revelation Seminars and the CHIP Seminar (the Coronary Health Improvement Project). The CHIP seminar ran for six weeks and was largely successful due to the members of Cornwall Church. Over nine hundred people signed up, and within three weeks, blood work was retaken and radical improvements in their cholesterol and blood sugar levels were seen. Also, by the end of the project our church raised several thousands of dollars to remodel and expand the church kitchen.

One cold, winter Sabbath morning, when the car heater should have been working, but wasn't, we had to scrape a few small spots on the inside windshield to see out. Finally arriving at the church, I ran into the building with our shoe bag and headed to the washroom. One can imagine how relieved I was to throw off my boots and thaw my toes on the heater vent. There was a soft knock on the door and Richard indicated he needed his shoes, tout de suite. Quickly I grabbed the shoe bag, and just as I was about to take them out, one of them slipped, and fell right into the toilet. I was horrified. I retrieved the wet shoe from the toilet and proceeded to wipe it off with paper towels, trying to appear calm. A minute later a second knock came, reminding me that Richard was anxious to have his shoes, because he had to be on the church platform immediately. Without informing him why one shoe was wet, I reluctantly opened the washroom door just enough to hand both shoes to him. As he quickly slipped them on, an odd expression came over his face, as I whispered some reassuring words, "Honey you will never walk the same again." I can still see him walking forward with his head turned around to face me, a puzzled expression written all over his face, and the background music of the "swishing shoe" as he marched away.

Throughout our ministry we enjoyed attending some of the provincial ministerial meetings that were held twice a year. We looked forward to renewing our friendships, sharing stories, and listening to guest speakers who had spiritual messages of hope and encouragement. There was one such time at one of our ministerial meetings that I recall quite vividly. It was in mid winter, and the meeting was held at Kingsway College in Oshawa, Ontario. As usual, my husband and I were looking forward to seeing our friends and having a special dinner together. Before the meal began the pastors and wives were all visiting around the room.

A gentleman whom we'd never before seen, came up to Richard and me holding his forehead and speaking fast. He said that he'd just flown in from the States and that he'd just gone to visit his close friend in Toronto. He'd discovered that his friend had AIDS and was quite shocked and distressed about his friend's prognosis. As soon as he said that, he asked us if we had an aspirin for his splitting headache. Richard found a few headache tablets and a glass of water to give him. The man thanked him, and went to the other side of the room to speak to someone. Meanwhile, Richard and I glanced sideways at one another and commented that perhaps this gentleman was homosexual, since his close friend was dying of AIDS.

A few minutes later we were all invited to sit at our tables and begin to eat. During desert, the president of the Ontario Conference approached the microphone and told us to continue eating while he introduced the guest speaker, Clifford Goldstein. As he came to the podium, Richard and I almost choked on our desert. Here stood the same man who'd told us about his close friend with AIDS, and how terribly stressful this was for him. He was also the man with the splitting headache who needed an aspirin. Here we assumed that since this man's friend was dying of AIDS, he must be gay himself.

I read a few of Clifford Goldstein's books and really found them interesting, but we'd never met him or seen a picture of him before the ministerial meeting. I believe we learned a valuable lesson that night, not to assume something about someone we don't even know.

"Life's disappointments are veiled love's appointments" by C.A. Fox

CHAPTER 18

ROMANIA

While living in Brockville and the Cornwall area, we decided to adopt a boy. We already had our miracle daughter who brought us lots of joy and an abundance of surprises. This hope for adopting a boy had been on our hearts for several years. We'd attempted various adoption avenues, including hospitals and Children's Aid, and finally we decided to try private adoption. We had friends, Pastor Dennis and Marlene Heinz, who were planning to adopt privately in Romania. They'd waited twenty-one years to have their own child, without results. The lady flew to Romania from Ottawa in March, 1991, and we kept in touch with her there. She gave us up-to-date details of what was going on in private adoptions and orphanages. In the meantime, we began doing the legal paperwork that needed to be processed by the social worker no later than the end of May. Then the Ministry of Community and Social Services had to receive all these documents, signed by lawyers. The adoption desk in Toronto told us that because of the backlog of adoption applications to Romania, it would take nine weeks to process ours. We appealed to their administrator to push our documents through as soon as possible, because judging by the update from friends in Romania, private adoptions in that country might close sooner than September 1991.

Apparently, the communist government was trying to shut down private adoption because of complaints about parents selling their children on the black market to foreigners. When the news of a possible shutdown hit the media in June 1991, our friend called to warn us. She had successfully adopted a child, but was still in Romania. On the media they announced a shut down of all foreign adoptions, but didn't announce a deadline. No one knew when that would take place. In the meantime, we sent all our available documents to Bucharest. We were still waiting on the final papers. When at last Toronto decided to release them a few weeks earlier than expected, Richard booked his flight to Romania.

There were times during this adoption roller coaster ride we felt like we just wanted to give up. With a time difference of seven hours between Romania and Ontario, a lack of sleep for almost four months, and so much red tape, we were feeling weary. Also, our new contact person in Romania would be cut off by the telephone company there, if she spoke to us in English. This became very frustrating because we couldn't connect with her sometimes for five days. The government would disconnect the phone line of any Romanian calling foreigners, if they thought the calls were too frequent. Tension was mounting for us. We had much at **stake** financially, invested time, and in trails of paperwork. This could all be lost if private adoption was closed.... perhaps even while Richard was airborne.

Our friend in Romania had recommended that Richard hide his extra cash inside his shoes. The government soldiers guarded the airport and searched any foreigner they thought might be coming to adopt a child. If the soldiers found cash, it would be temporarily confiscated. Richard and I packed dry soups, toys, little bags of dried fruits, and even colored icicles in his suitcase to give to the Christian Romanian couple with whom he'd be staying.

Upon his arrival at Bucharest, Richard was met by our Canadian friend who would be leaving for Canada shortly. The Romanian couple he'd be staying with also met him. The next day, at the president's office for adoption, Richard handed over the remaining documents from Toronto. He was able to speak French with this Romanian official. When the president looked at the papers, which had been translated into Romanian, he sharply told Richard that private adoption had ended a few days before, on July 16th. It was too late to adopt any child. Richard was caught off guard, but he didn't give up, pleading with the official to reconsider. Apparently, the other documents that had been sent to his office in June had been overlooked and weren't stamped. Richard explained to him how the mother of this two-year old child had consented to have us adopt her son. He also gave him the mother's letter dated and stamped months before by their office. Richard tried to appeal to the president's heart by telling him how the two-year old boy had to stay home alone everyday, while his mother went to school. The official finally said, "Don't you have laws in Canada?"

Richard said, "Of course we do, but our people are usually made aware of any major changes long in advance, before a law is passed." Richard considered offering the president a bribe to see if that would work, but thought better of it, in case he ended up in prison. It was pointless to pursue the matter further with the president. Richard had to accept his final answer. When he had a chance to call me and tell me the sad news, I was in shock. My heart felt so heavy and burdened that it was difficult to concentrate on anything else. Our future plans for this child were gone forever. Even to this day, I carry the little two-year-old boy's picture in my wallet. Today I've reconciled to the fact that itwas God's plan all along for us not to have this adoption succeed. "All things work together for good to those who love God."

Often I reflect on my childhood. Despite the continual conflict in my home, mountains of struggles, and the insecurities that filled my life, the cushion of love that my mother provided for me was never pulled out from me completely. Without these scars which brought at times deep pains, I would never had wanted Jesus to be part of my life. He bore the deepest scars of all. Regardless of the uncharted territory of my past, I know for certainty that God's charted territory is safe and sure for the present and the future.

Since Richard still had two weeks left in Romania, he kept approaching different people who might be able to help him. He was learning the Romanian language quickly, and could shop on his own easily. When he gave the couple where he was staying the dry soups, icicles, dried fruits and toys, he was amazed by what they liked the most. The icicles were a grand success and they liked the dry soup, but they did not like the taste of the dried fruits, even though fresh fruits are rarely seen in the supermarkets. People who had farms grew their own apples, but city folks did without. Once a year they could queue up to buy bananas. Fruit was definitely a luxury. Of all the things my husband brought to share with this couple who were in their twenties, the plastic toys were the biggest hit. This surprised my husband who was going to suggest they give the toys to their nephews. The Romanian man told Richard that he remembers receiving a toy only when he was around twelve years old.

While he was there, Richard was asked to give a sermon in one of the largest Christian churches of our denomination in that country. Over 1500 people attended and everyone wanted to shake his hand which eventually became quite numb. The people seemed very receptive and kind. Through an interpreter, they expressed their thankfulness for his gospel-centered message that burnt in their hearts. They were surprised to see that Richard hardly looked at his notes while speaking and they asked how he did that. Apparently, when the Romanian President Ceausescu was in power and the Orthodox Church ran the country, no preacher was allowed to memorize his sermon for the pulpit. He had to write it word for word and hand it to an official, before he was scheduled to speak at church. Each week, a communist official would come with a copy of the sermon and make sure the preacher was reading it word for word. God has changed all that, temporarily at least, and the power of His Word is growing in leaps and bounds in Romania, just like in the Biblical day of Pentecost.

While Richard was off in Romania, Rachelle and I spent time with our family in Cambridge and the most unusual thing happened at my sister Nadine's house. We were invited to swim in their pool and enjoy the day. My other sister Sandy was making refreshments in the house to bring out to the pool area. Unbeknowned to anyone our brother-in-law, Bill, forgot to place some heavy stones in the bottom of the table with the umbrella attached to it. Unfortunately, a heavy wind swept by and caught the table and umbrella and the drinks that were on the table moments later, and it all landed in the pool on top of Rachelle, our daughter who was about 10 years old. Immediately I jumped in the pool and pushed the table and umbrella away from Rachelle. Unfortunately, we noticed that Nadine's new cellphone ended up in the water as well. After retrieving all of these items a stack of valuable papers and documents that belonged to Nadine were floating in the pool. Now these papers were no ordinary papers, they belonged to her employer, who was the Member of Provincial Parliament. She had to work on them for the next day.

What a surprise awaited Nadine when she came home from collecting her daughter, Andrea, at school. On the fence around the pool were these important wet papers pasted to the fence. When she discovered that her new cellphone was water logged and ruined she felt overwhelmed. In the meantime, Bill was in the dog house when Nadine went looking for him. She found him in one of the washrooms muttering to himself mopping up water that overflowed from the toilet.

We all agreed that after this catastrophe we could alleviate our frustrations by eating at a local quain restaurant. Once we found the ideal place, an outside café, we sat at a table with an attached umbrella. In the meanwhile, we noticed that Bill was sitting at another table alone with a look of chagrin written all over his face. Suddenly a gust of wind blew across the umbrella Bill was sitting under, which collapsed right on his head. He just sat there, a surrendered victim to the collapsible umbrella, staring in space, not caring what happened next. Anyway, so much for living in the dog house.

Before leaving this district, we had a royal experience when Prince Charles and Princess Diana came to Kingston, Ontario, about an hour's drive from us, on a royal visit to Canada. Upon our late arrival, the church school children and teacher found a comfortable spot among the mass of people to hopefully sneak a view of the royal couple; while Richard perched himself far up on a tree to video the couples exiting the Royal Britannia Ship on the St. Lawrence Seaway. Then I was alone praying to God to find me a perfect view and it seemed before my eyes a small pathway opened up and I quickly found myself on the front row behind a short gate facing Prince Charles. He was awaiting Princess Diana who was still down the line greeting the people and children who gave gifts of flowers and stuffed animals to the princess. I assumed since Prince Charles had nothing else to do but wait he began a conversation with me.

His first words to me was, "Is it always this cold this time of the year in Canada?" I was a little taken back that he was speaking directly to me and I responded by saying, " The end of October is the beginning of colder weather, and the change from Autumn to the beginning of Winter can be felt. He must have noticed everyone wearing winter coats and realized that we were prepared and used to the weather change. It seemed apparent that the royal couple were wearing light jackets and weren't expecting this much cold in October.

His conversation was pleasant as he commented on the crowd of people present, despite the cold weather. For some reason I forgot to take a photo of him even though a camera hung around my neck. Suddenly the atmosphere changed as the crowd began to cheer loudly when Princess Diana made her way down the line close to where I stood. It felt like the Beatle mania as the people applauded, with strong whistles and cheers ascending in the air. For some reason Prince Charles wasn't given that strong of a welcome.

Being aware of the tabloid rumours that the royal couple were separating, and that they probably wouldn't poise for a photo together I gingerly replied to Prince Charles, "would you mind stepping aside while I take Prince Diana's photo." He eagerly obeyed and said, "certainly, certainly as he stepped back". I felt so crude and impolite, "What have I done to speak like that to the Prince of Wales, I can't not look at him in the face ever again I'm so embarrassed." Finally the princess was face to face with me as I clumsily snapped her picture. She then made a pivot turn toward the designated Cadillac vehicle without as much as a glance at Prince Charles. To this day I still look back at this awesome event as a royal moment, despite the fact my husband jokingly commented, "For all we know your bossey attitude toward Prince Charles might have caused the royal couple to divorce."

"Victory is gained only through conflict" by Al Berstein

CHAPTER 19

A NARROW ESCAPE IN RUSSIA

It was one of those weeks where so much was happening that one needed roller blades to keep up with our deadlines. We were transferring to another district and had to leave behind our unsold house. Sounds like a broken record. That particular week, my husband was already working in the new district and I was home packing boxes, cleaning the house, and keeping it neat and tidy for the viewers whom the realtor brought.

On the day of our move to Barrie, Richard had to drop me off in Toronto, on his way to the new district in the moving truck. There were still more Family Life courses I needed to take in order to complete my Family Life Educator certificate from Andrews University. I stayed in Toronto for ten days, doing a lot of class work and homework. Of course, my mind was on my family in our new home, unpacking boxes, including one hundred-fifty boxes of Richard's books. This was my second time leaving my family on a moving day, to take courses, but timing isn't always the way we plan.

Well into the week, a few of my friends who were taking the same course, mentioned to me that they were planning to go to Russia. They were part of a team of youth and a couple of Family Life directors who'd be spending five weeks in Moscow, during August and September, in 1994. My heart's desire was to be part of that team too, and I prayed about it. The week sped by and we were ready to say farewell to our class and head home, me to unpack boxes in our new district. Just as I was about to depart, I went up to our teachers to thank them for their teaching expertise.. Suddenly, I was impressed to ask if they needed another person to join their group on the Russian trip. The director said he would find out and then get back to me in a few weeks.

What a spring to remember. In May, we had moved into our fourth home in eight years. We had a Christian lady living with us in our previous districts, and she was moving with us to Barrie. Unfortunately, due to her special needs, she had become ill, and had to be hospitalized on the day of our move. The same month, my mother, who'd had been living in Florida took ill, and my brother Gregory, Nadine and I went down to Florida for a week to sell her house and bring her back home. Then in June, my husband, Richard, myself, and our daughter Rachelle, traveled to Canadian University College in Alberta for his alumni weekend. We drove all the way to Alberta from Ontario which was over 2,000 miles. In July, I attended the Family Life Educator ceremony at Andrews in Michigan, where I graduated with a Family Life Educator Certificate, and completed this spiritual-filled weekend with a scrumptuous banquet. Then in August, I was preparing to go to Russia.

A few months before my trip some friends asked us if we wouldn't mind taking care of their two children who were around our daughter, Rachelle's age. The parents were having to travel overseas on church business for a week. Of course, we looked forward to the opportunity of having them.

The next morning children arrived at the bus station in Barrie where Richard picked them up. They arrived from Florida where they spent part of their summer vacations with relatives. We then packed our van for a vacation to our rustic cabin in Quebec, Canada, and everyone, including, Ivan and Sara were looking forward to fishing, boating and having a relaxing fun time.

Finally we were almost finished loading the van, when Sara approached me with a concerned look on her face, and her finger pointing to her head. She said that her head was itching terribly, and she couldn't stop scratching it. Not thinking that it was very serious I took a look at her head and found these little black critters jumping up and down looked like they were on a trampaline. At that moment, all I could think of is "It can't be lice, surely not....just when we were packed and going out the door." The reality of what had to be done to get rid of lice, not only from Sara's thick long hair, but how contagious lice is...for they are no respecter of people and love to share their nests of eggs with everyone they come across,....made my head spin.

At that point, we reluctantly took out our packed suitcases from the van realizing we had to postpone our trip to our cabin. Our first priority was to wash all the clothes, and bed sheets first and run to the pharmacy for lice shampoo and a lice comb. Since Richard volunteered to start loading the sheets first in the washing machine, I went to the pharmacy to purchase the necessary items. When I returned Richard was taking the sheets out of the washing machine to put in the drier, when I noticed red streaks all over the white sheets, which were not there before.

Upon questioning further he said that he threw in some red items, and a few coloured shirts in with the sheets to save time. At that moment I knew that I should have been doing the washing while he ran to the pharmacy. It's obvious who took over the washing after that experience.

After shampooing and scrubbing all the heads, starting with Sara first, the following day we left on our trip with eagerness. No sooner did we arrive at our cabin, everybody gladly jumped out of the van, while Richard and his willing helpers took the boat out of the shed, and whoever wanted to fish jumped in the boat. Since I am not a fisher woman I volunteered to put away the groceries and make up the beds with the streaked red and white sheets.

There were no other mishaps for the following few days as we enjoyed our time relaxing as the children prepared the fish in a batter of a pancake mix cooked in a frying pan on a wooden stove. Nothing tastes better than food cooked on a wooden stove. How delicious that is.

Even our weather was cooperating as the much needed sun shone brightly everyday.

Since we were expecting Sara and Ivan's parents to join us for the last phrase of our vacation, we planned to meet them, and then return to our rustic cabin again so that we all could be together and enjoy another few days.

On the second day at our cabin everyone except one person were scratching their heads. Out came the lice and comb and we all ran to the lake in long rubber boots to shampoo our heads once again. For the next three days we spent our time washing and drying clothes at the laundry facility in town thirty miles away. Guess how we spent our nights? In the water with flash lights, rubber boots and lice shampoo washing our heads. Then we would come back to the cabin around 11 p.m. and started cooking our supper which was usually Chinese noodle soup and sandwiches. After eating we quickly did up the dishes, and crawled into bed around 1p.m. and at 6a.m. sharp Richard was up putting wood in the stove to take away the chill in the air, and promptly jumped in the boat with his gear to catch fish for breakfast around 10 a.m. Whoever wanted to join him had to get up quickly, dress, and run to the boat.

Richard and I apologized so many times to our friends for this crazy time we all experienced, but they didn't want to hear about it. Apparently, according to them, they had the best time they had in years. They immensely enjoyed the laughter, fishing, boating, and even the late nights spent in the lake shampooing our heads. It was the quality of friendship, and their Christian attitude that made all the difference.

After our unusual vacations it was time to pack for my five week trip to Russia. It was good that our coordinators were in touch with me, advising me what to bring, including the type of subjects I'd be speaking on. Of course, they were family orientated talks. Also, we were asked to bring dry foods , such as soup, crackers, rice and so on. Souvenirs and gifts were welcomed and we gave out a lot of souvenirs to the Russian people and children. I brought treats like gum, little toys, shampoo, soaps and many trinkets. Our co-ordinator told me that my talks would include giving parenting seminars, and seminars relating to the unbelieving spouse. However, something impressed me to pack in my suitcase my New Age talk that I had recently given in our church districts, and at one university in Michigan.

Upon our arrival in Moscow, Russia, all of us felt very 'jet lagged' after having flown for over fourteen hours. We were relieved that we arrived safely at the crowded airport, which was quite small in comparison to our large airports in North America. Before communism fell, there was likely less traffic in and out of Russia, as compared to the traffic that had increased so much. It was obvious to see that the airport wasn't adequate to serve the vast throngs of people. A short time after our arrival at the Moscow airport, we spotted someone carrying a large sign that read, "Anyone from the SDA Church of North America, please see me." We were relieved to see that sign. The driver helped us through the crowd, and assisted us with our suitcases, and brought us to our destination safely. Did I say safely? The driving on the highways, and in the city of Moscow was so chaotic that it was a miracle we made it safely anywhere. If a bus was stopped at the traffic lights, this would not deter an impatient car driver behind the bus from passing it on the sidewalk.

We were able to take a three day break after our plane trip before starting into our speaking engagements. Our schedules were busy and many Russians were coming to all the various seminars and evangelistic meetings held at the Olympic Center, right across the street from the KGB's office.

While traveling on the bus, on the second night of our evangelistic meetings, I met an young eighteen-year old girl named Natalie. She spoke very good English, and by talking with her she mentioned she was a translator, but the company she worked for let her go. because they were cutting back on employers. Eager to invite her to the Evangelistic Crusade I told her there might be a need for a translator where I was to speak that evening. While praying that God could use this young lady, I approached my co-ordinator to ask if they could use another translator. His response was, "As a matter of fact, one of our youth translators became ill and we need to replace her this evening." Voila! God is so timely. She was able to work that evening and every night afterward. Also, she stayed with some of the female youth leaders in their apartment and they shared some Christian literature with her which she read. Remember,

Natalie never heard of the Bible or Jesus Christ our Saviour and Friend.

During the second week of the seminar, the buzz around the team volunteers was that they needed to give seminars on the New Age, since a lot of the new Christians from last years previous crusade had been involved in Hatha Yoga and meditation. A lot of the new converts had brought their Hindu philosophy with them when they became church members and continued to practice it. When my co-ordinator asked me if I knew of someone who might be able to assist him with the New Age seminar I was speechless. I had enough harassments from Satan and didn't want any more. But my friend who overheard the conversation volunteered me. The co-ordinator was East Indian and was quite able to explain the Hindu philosophy to these new converts, but he was looking for someone who had experienced it. I reluctantly agreed to help him.

Our directors gave us a three day break to travel and tour Russia, if we wanted to before beginning our last phase of the crusade. My new program would entail traveling by car to all the churches, conferences, and schools, including the Theology Seminary to speak of my New Age experience. Two other ladies, Bernice MacDonald and Jessie Francis from Toronto, a Russian interpreter and I, took the ten-hour night train from Moscow to St. Petersburg. After three days of exploring St. Peterburg, and its beautiful architecture, we began the return trip to Moscow. After three hours into our trip, I stooped down to get something from my suitcase when suddenly a drunken man jumped into our compartment, and threw me on the floor, and tried to tear off my clothes. I screamed out loud and managed to push him away. I surprised myself because he was a lot bigger and heavier than I was. My body was trembling, and my voice was shaking as I pleaded with our translator to ask him to leave. Finally he gave the drunk a strong nudge out our compartment door.

Because of this incident, I knew that Satan was behind it and wanted to discourage me from speaking about my experience with the New Age. It was getting quite late, but my heart was beating fast and sleep left me. All I could think about was how many more harassments would follow. I made up my mind not to speak about the New Age and inwardly told God my thoughts. But God wouldn't give up impressing on my heart and mind that if I went through with my talks, Satan would have no more hold on me and I would have victory over my personal attacks from Satan. A while later another impression and warning seemed to come to my mind through the Holy Spirit.

The strong thoughts that entered my mind indicated that in another seven hours there would be a further attack on my life, but I was not to fear it, because it would be the last time I'd be controlled by the Evil One. After those impressions I felt even stronger about not giving my talk about my New Age experience in Moscow, Russia.

At that moment I felt like Jonah in the belly of the fish trying to run away from God. About seven hours later we got off the train in Moscow and caught a bus to return to our apartment. On the bus we showed our tickets to the conductor, but we forgot to punch them on the wall puncher, and broke a rule that we had forgotten about. We sat close to the back of the bus and I was in deep thought and still struggling with my refusal to do what God wanted me to do. At that moment we heard a loud voice that seemed to be coming from the front of the bus. There stood a huge man speaking in a loud voice in Russian, and appeared very upset about something. Gradually he began walking towards the back. At that moment, I remembered the un-punched tickets that could lead to a fine, because passengers who forget to punch their tickets are breaking the law. Since my friend Jessie was holding our tickets, I quickly mentioned to her to quickly punch them. As she approached the puncher, the angry man pushed her hand away. Then he came up to me, grabbed me by the neck, and threw me off the bus. I landed on my face on the ground. I was just glad that the bus was already stationary before I flew in the air, and landed with a thump. With scraped knees, a sore neck and back, and a hurt pride, I looked up from the ground toward the sky and said, "All right Lord I'll do it. I'll do the New Age seminar regardless of what happens to me." Meanwhile, the shouting man jumped off the bus and demanded money from us for disobeying the law. We paid our fine and I limped to our apartment glad to be still alive.

Day and night my co-ordinator and I were taxied to our different churches, conferences, and schools throughout Moscow. My co-ordinator explained the history of Hinduism while I talked about my experience in the New Age. A peace enveloped me wherever I went. I truly knew that victory in Christ was finally mine. Ever since that dark frightful evening in St. Petersburg, I've never been harassed by Satan. God kept His promise and replaced my fear with His peace in that far-away country. I came back home a different person than when I left.

Another church move was set, but this time it was to be to another the province of British Columbia. With had such fond memories of our four years spent in our church in Barrie. This time it was difficult to move away from our family and friends.

However, before we took a call to Williams Lake District in British Columbia, Richard received a message from Mrs. Cameron, a member who Richard baptized several years ago, from our previous church in Cornwall. She mentioned that her daughter from Atlanta, Georgia, was getting married and would like Richard to marry them at her home, near Cornwall, off the St. Lawrence River. This request seemed a little unusual since Richard never met Mrs. Cameron's daughter and husband to be before the wedding date. However, Richard was very fond of Mrs. Cameron who was elderly. He reassured her that he would get in touch with her daughter and fiancé to arrange for their wedding.

On the weekend of the wedding Mrs. Cameron called and told us that she had a motel reserved for us, and so we met her at this motel. When we arrived at this cosy looking motel, Mrs. Cameron showed us inside our room. We noticed that her daughter had all these different beautifully wrapped gifts for us on the various beds and tables. It seemed that the daughter was some kind of mystery woman that we still hadn't met yet.

On the day of the wedding we drove down the road toward Mrs. Camerons home We weren't sure if we knew exactly where Mrs. Cameron's home was because we moved out of the district several years ago, and we unfortunately, forgot her address back at the hotel.

In this area most of these gorgeous homes all faced the St. Lawrence River. Half way down we noticed a large home where a wedding was taking place. We got out of our vehicle and made our way to the backyard where there stood a large tent full of chairs, decorations, and food. What a spectacular view! It was facing the different sailboats on the St. Lawrence River. When we arrived at the tent we stood there looking inside trying to spot the unknown woman and groom of the wedding for what seemed a long time. Time was marching on, and still we couldn't find the wedding couple, nor Mrs. Cameron. We continued to search for any familiar faces, and were getting a little anxious when we couldn't find anyone we knew.

Finally we couldn't take it any longer so we agreed to ask some one if they knew the mother of the bride, and also the wedding couple. Then from the corner of our eyes a red car pulled up near the home and asked if there was a Pastor Richard Parent present. When Richard heard his name being called, he was a little curious as he approached the red car. A lady exit her car , and quickly asked him, "Are you Pastor Parent?" as he nodded in the affirmative. She seemed relieved and continued speaking. She said, "Pastor Parent I believe you are at the wrong wedding! Would you please follow me, because the wedding couple that you are supposed to be marrying is anxiously waiting for you a few houses down the road."

"A Bible that is falling apart usually belongs to someone who isn't." By Theodore Roszak

CHAPTER 20

THE WEST COAST CALLS US

Another move was in store for us far away from Ontario to the city of Williams Lake, in the interior of British Columbia. Williams Lake is a small town with caribou, bears, and cougars roaming the nearby forests. Some of the cougars often came into town, and there are stories of people barely escaping with their lives as cougars become aggressive when hungry. There was a story about one man killed by a cougar in Williams Lake.

Williams Lake is a place of majestic mountains that overlook a lake right in the heart of the town. Lots of ranchers with large herds of cattle are spread throughout the area. Sometimes these cattle wander across small country roads and if they decide to lie down on the road, so be it. Drivers have to watch carefully to avoid hitting them, or face a $5,000 fine. Some of our friends own a hobby ranch, where we were invited one Sunday. They planned to brand some cattle and asked Richard and Rachelle if they'd like to learn. They agreed to try it. However, at one point, as they were pinning down one of the steers, Richard got kicked in the ribs and was quite sore for a time. It was a good reminder not to take up ranching as a career.

We soon bonded with the William's Lake church members and participated in a lot of socials. We were kept busy with ministry and outreach programs. I eventually enrolled in university psychology courses which I thoroughly enjoyed. Richard was doing his doctorate of theology dissertation by correspondence from the University of South Africa. He completed this program in December 2003.

One Sunday we took a brief visit to Barkerville, one of the popular gold rush towns from the nineteenth century. We took in historical sites, including the old general shops, clothing stores, hotels and the theater's slapstick comedy of the Wild West. I didn't get an opportunity to pan for gold there. However, I had a different type of experience searching for gold not long afterward.

I chipped an old tooth at the back of my mouth. In consultation with the dentist, I decided to go for my very first "gold crowned tooth". A temporary crown was put on the old tooth, while I waited two weeks for the gold crown to be made.

Returning to the dentist, I felt a brief nervous twitch in my stomach however, I settled back in the chair as he explained the procedure. The moment finally came when the dentist removed the temporary crown and replaced it with a permanent gold one. It seemed that the crown was a little tight and the dentist tried to adjust it, but couldn't. Finally, he decided to take the gold crown out, and have it sent off for further adjustment. As he carefully removed it from my mouth, it slipped from his fingers. I wasn't aware of this, but since some little particles were floating around inside my mouth and water was being sprayed also, I swallowed. The dentist asked me to give him back the gold crown, thinking it was still in my mouth.

I bolted upright from the chair, like a cadaver in a coffin, as the reality hit home that I'd swallowed more than a few particles. Reluctantly I looked at the dentist's ashen face, which confirmed that same reality. To my chagrin, I heard him say, "Don't worry, once you RETRIEVE the gold crown from your system, it will be sterilized for about ten minutes, and fitted into your mouth. It will look as good as new. It's like drinking recycled water...a piece of cake."

But I was in a state of shock. I gagged on the word RETRIEVE. The dentist went on to explain that it would take two to three days before the gold crown would be out of my system. I wasn't very comforted by this. However, I tried to look on the bright side. After all, this would be my first attempt at panning for gold.

Not having any experience in this area, I equipped myself with a plastic medium-sized pail and rubber gloves and went to work. I wasn't sure if it was psychological or physical, but this ordeal triggered my mild state of colitis and I was making more trips to the toilet than planned. My husband and daughter kept encouraging me by singing their favorite tune, "There's gold in them there stools." After a few days of finding no gold in the pail, I switched to a smaller bowl, thinking surely I wouldn't miss it. Still no gold to be found. Then out of desperation, I chose a small strainer. Yes, a kitchen strainer. After six days of searching with no trace of the gold crown, I finally made an appointment at the local hospital to have an x-ray taken.

I arrived at the hospital with a form from my doctor, requesting an x-ray of my stomach and intestines. However, after briefly explaining my circumstances to the nurse, she began to laugh uncontrollably. Then an announcement came over the PA to vacate the property because a fire had been discovered in the hospital. That meant that all of us who were mobile had to walk off the hospital premises. A few minutes later another announcement declared it a false alarm. This was turning out to be a real "hair day". Finally the x-ray was taken and it revealed no gold crown. Not long afterwards I returned to the same dentist's office, and settled for a porcelain tooth instead of a gold crown, and not just for esthetic reasons. The very thought of having gold in my mouth turned me off. Funny, I haven't the faintest idea why.

It seemed that the two years we spent in British Columbia went too fast. We had a lot of adventure and wonderful times however, we felt a call from God back to the ministry in Ontario. It was difficult leaving our fond friends behind. We will always cherish the time we spent in Williams Lake, especially the experience of panning for gold. Since Richard's father had passed away recently, he wanted to be near his mother and family. In fact, we both had a deep desire to return to Hamilton where our families resided.

Richard became pastor of the Heritage Church and chaplain of the Heritage Nursing Home. Coming home at last, created in me a desire to share more time with my family. My siblings were a very important part of my growing-up years and I desired it to be so again

"A true missionary is God's man in God's place, doing God's work in God's way for God's glory" by Eleanor Doan

CHAPTER 21

FROM THE FREEZER INTO THE FRYING PAN

Empathetically, I told the Lord that there were three things that I would never do: (1), drive my car through busy Toronto traffic, (2) preach, (3) take a call to Africa. I ended up doing all three.

It soon became evident that God had other plans for us. In January 2000, our daughter Rachelle decided she wanted to attend our Adventist Academy and be a missionary in Eastern Africa. So, at the age of sixteen she left Canada and flew to Nairobi, Kenya. There she enrolled in Maxwell Academy, a Christian American school, to complete her high school. As parents, we had many doubts and some regrets as to whether we'd done the right thing by letting her go all the way to Africa. Frightful thoughts kept popping up in our minds about her safety, her adjustments to another culture, her young age, and so on. We could only give her to the Lord, asking Him to put a hedge around her and keep her from harm.

We received daily e-mails and weekly telephone calls from Rachelle. She sounded very positive and exuberant about her new adventure. She had a part-time job working in the cafeteria in the early mornings. On weekends she and other students would sign up to visit different children's hospitals' that dealt with children with AIDS. The students' hearts were burdened with what they saw. Several children died, innocent victims of this horrible disease. There were also scheduled weekends where foreign parents organized student excursion campouts, and projects such as students volunteering to build huts for the tall Masai African tribe. Apparently, this tribe was superstitious about digging beneath the ground to build their huts and other small buildings, because they feared the evil spirits would rise up and hurt them. Rachelle was part of these projects and really felt she was contributing to the needy tribe. They also built relationships with the community. In time, we began to feel relieved and no longer regretted sending her to Kenya.

In June, 2000, the General Conference Session was held in Toronto, Ontario. Every five years the General Conference Session takes place in the United States or Europe. However, this was the first time it was held in Canada. Richard and I signed up as volunteers to work at the front desk of the Ontario Convention Center where the sessions were held. There were over 70,000 Adventists from all over the world who attended this great celebration.

The last week of the program, Richard and I were interviewed by the president of the Sahel Union of West Africa. They were seeking a bilingual pastor who spoke both French and English to be employed as president of the Burkina Faso Seventh-day Adventist Mission. The General Conference was the employer, and the term was for six years. After listening to the interviewer explaining the job, Richard spoke first and said that he would be happy to take the call, but his wife did not feel the same as he did. Then he glanced at me for some acknowledgment so I began by asking the president several questions . "Are there poisonous snakes in Burkina Faso?" The president explained that there are snakes, but mainly in the far off villages, and since we would be stationed in the large city there were none. Then I asked more questions and received reasonable answers. At that moment, I recalled two other times in our ministry when we'd received overseas calls to Africa, and they hadn't materialized. I was thinking that when God called us this third time, we'd better go or we would disappoint Him. Richard couldn't believe my next statement. But these words actually came out of my mouth. "As reluctant as I am, my husband would like to experience mission service, and so I want to please him and God at the same time."

Before we left Canada, we searched the internet for background information about Burkina Faso. This is what we discovered.

The population of Burkina Faso in 2002 was 12,603,185, but it increased to 14,326,203 by 2007. This is the third poorest country in the world and its inhabitants are afflicted with a high mortality rate from AIDS as well as food or waterborne diseases: bacterial and protozoal diarrhea, hepatitis A, and typhoid fever, along with respiratory diseases like meningitis. Many deaths are also due to malaria.

The country's official language is French, but people generally speak one of the thirty-four tribal languages. Formerly the Republic of Upper Volta, it was renamed on August 4, 1984 by President Thomas Sankara to mean, the land of upright people, (or, upright land,) in Mossi and Dioula, the major native languages of the country.

During the long summer, the dry dusty Sahara desert temperature climbs 130 degrees Fahrenheit, or 55 degrees Celsius in the day, and a low of 100 degrees Fahrenheit or 38 degrees Celsius at night. What we observed about the rainy seasons, in the two years we lived in the city of Ouagadougou, was that it rarely rained. For the most part, drought exists everywhere in that area of Africa.

An American Adventist couple, Pastor John and Ruby Stafford, whom we met briefly at the General Conference Session in July, explained that they'd been asked to come to Burkina Faso and hold a crusade in the large church where we would attend. They were not sure if they were going; they seemed undecided. If they did go, they said they would leave around the same time that we did in November, 2000. That's why it was a happy surprise to see them at the Paris, France, airport. The Staffords had been missionaries during the genocide episode in Rwanda. We felt very fortunate to have them with us for three weeks. They were encouraging in helping us break new turf. Also, they were good company, since Richard had to attend a ministerial meeting in the next country of Togo shortly after we arrived in Burkina Faso.

When we did arrive at the Ouagadougou airport, there were several Adventist people there to meet us, including the foreign ADRA Director, Allain Long. They quickly took our suitcases and drove us to our new home. It was very late when we arrived so we didn't unpack until the next morning. It was planned ahead of time that we would hire a housekeeper and cook for the time we would be living in Burkina Faso. We understood that hiring a maid would help feed her family, and educate her children. Marion, a Burkinabé, was a very hard and reliable worker. In the past there had been different foreign presidents of the Adventist mission, who'd lived in the compound house, and Marion had been their housekeeper and cook as well, so she had learned how to cook Brazilian, Dutch, American, and now some French Canadian cuisine.

I never thought before we arrived in Ouagadougou, West Africa, just what kind of work the Lord wanted me to do. But after two days of being there, I didn't have to wonder any longer.

A Zambian lady named Beauty and her five children showed up at our mission gate. She explained in good English that she was homeless with no money. She apparently was a Christian Adventist but no longer practiced her religion, because she'd married a strict Muslim who wouldn't allow her to do so. She had many regrets from her marriage to a Muslim. He was her second husband and when she married him in Zambia, she already had two small children from her previous marriage. Then they had three children together. The Muslim husband became a dictator and controlled every move and idea that Beauty would suggest. Finally, he forced her and the children to leave her beloved country of Zambia, and move to a hot desert in Mali, situated north of Burkina Faso, to live a Muslim life. This man and his family were very abusive. In fact, he kidnaped Beauty's two oldest children and placed them with his relatives that lived in another part of Mali, where Beauty wouldn't find them.

It became very difficult to live under his strict regime, and Beauty prayed to God for many years that she and the children could return safely to Zambia. One day she decided to stop rebelling against her husband's religion and pretended to be an obedient, submissive Muslim wife. She deeply missed her two other children who had been gone for several years now, because she wouldn't surrender to the Islamic faith. After months of playing the submissive wife, her husband began to relax, and didn't mind if she and the three children went on walks, or even went to purchase food items. At last, she found out where her other two children were and when everyone was attending a village celebration, she escaped with her five children and ended up at our mission gate. After hearing Beauty's soft voice pleading for help, I knew that God would use me somehow to find support for her and the children. I began to pray in my heart for guidance.

After settling them in a hut furnished with everything they needed, one of the first things we did was go to the Ghana Embassy by taxi, to see if they could help Beauty obtain a visa. It was amusing to experience taking a taxi as a foreigner. Beauty and I flagged down the taxi and bartered with the driver for a reasonable price. Unknown to us, the locals wait along the roads, and when a foreigner climbs into a taxi, about six of them jump in as well. They all want a free ride to wherever we are going. Upon arriving at the Ghana Embassy and waiting two hours to speak to a representative, we found them uncooperative.

One day, a week after Beauty's appearance, the Baptist minister called our mission and I took the call. He told me that about a week ago a lady by the name of Beauty and her children had visited his mission for assistance. Before he promised help, he'd asked her if she would become a member of his Baptist church if they helped her? She immediately replied in her soft spoken voice, " I was raised an Adventist, and even though I have strayed from my church, I plan to return and be re-baptized." The minister said that he understood how sincere and spiritual she was and promised that he would see what he could do. Well, his telephone call was encouraging. He said that there was a retired, rich ambassador in his church, who would be willing to take Beauty and all her five children to the English speaking country of Ghana, in his brand new limousine. Ghana is about a ten hour drive from Burkina Faso. If our ADRA Director would be willing to keep them for awhile perhaps money could be raised to fly her and the children back to Zambia.

I found that this Baptist minister was a devoted tither. He told me his story about how he became associated with our Adventist Church in Burkin Faso. He said about ten years before he'd been asked to translate from English into French at an Evangelistic Crusade that our Adventist church had. The American evangelist needed a translator. When the evangelist spoke about the Biblical tithing system, the Baptist minister was quite happy to discover this Bible principle and after the crusade, he spoke for a long time with the evangelist about it. He was totally convinced that tithing was Biblical and he returned to his church and taught them how to do it. His last comment was that he and his congregation returned to God a faithful tithe.

When John and Ruby Stafford held evangelistic meetings in French in our church, Beauty and her five children were baptized. One of Beauty's request' was to have an English Bible to study God's Word. for herself. Beauty and a member of the church went to the publishing house that day and purchased English Bibles for Beauty and her children. When the Bibles were given to Beauty, her face looked radiant as she expressed her appreciation.

The Staffords and Richard and I gave money for Beauty and her children to take on their trip to Ghana. In the meantime, I sent a letter to the Director of ADRA with Beauty and explained why she must leave Burkina Faso. First of all, she and her children didn't know how to speak French. Secondly, they didn't have a legal visa, and, most importantly, her Muslim husband was searching for her. We requested that they get special care, food supplies and medical treatment, if possible.

Not long after they left, we received a harsh reply from the ADRA Director in Ghana stating that it was wrong for the President of the Burkina Faso Mission to send a desperate, single mother and children to them.

In January we received a telephone call from Beauty who was now back home in Zambia with her five children. She had filed for divorce and obtained a restraining order against her Muslin husband. She sounded very happy and extended her appreciation to all of us. At the end of the conversation she mentioned how the Staffords had taken a bank loan from their American bank back home, to pay the air fare back to Zambia for her and the children. My trust and faith in God grew stronger from hearing Beauty's testimony. Does Jesus really care? In the NIV, Psalm 116:1 it says, "I love the Lord, because he listens to my prayers for help, He paid attention to me, so I will call to him for help as long as I live."

After the Staffords left for United States, I was hired as Richard's part-time secretary in the Mission office. Obviously, I didn't have to wonder for very long what God had planned for me to do.

CHAPTER 22

A CHRISTMAS EVE TRAUMA

December 24, 2000, is printed boldly across my mind. Who could have known what this day would hold? Richard was to perform his first Adventist wedding at Bobo, a six hour car drive from Ouagadougou, Burkina Faso. Local Adventists had warned him not to drive at night because it was too dangerous. Donkey carts, animals and broken-down vehicles spread out all over the roads. But Richard went and a young African man wear with him, an active Adventist member from our local church. The wedding was delayed until later in the day, so Richard and Michael were driving back in the dark. Richard was supposed to meet Rachelle, our daughter, my niece Andrea, and me at a French couple's place for supper at 9:30 a.m. Christmas Eve. When it got quite late and he hadn't called or shown up, we all became concerned. Around 1:30a.m., Christmas morning, the telephone rang. The caller was from the General Hospital in Ouagadougou where we lived. He explained about a Richard Parent who'd been in a very serious car accident around 8:30p.m., December 24, and was at the General Hospital. We had our security guard drive us to the hospital, Rachelle and my niece Andrea ran ahead of us and found Richard full of blood lying in a small cot. It was a gory sight to behold. Before I reached my husband though, I had to step over several dead bodies lying on the floor. Then I recognized Michael, the passenger who'd gone with Richard, sprawled on the floor. He whispered to me that he was thirsty, and I noticed blood flowing from his mouth. Of course, I didn't know the seriousness of his injury at that moment. What we didn't discover until two weeks later was that on Christmas Eve, a police officer was on his way to another accident scene when he saw Richard smash into a immobile broken down army truck that was placed on the road without any flashers, or signs. Only a long broken branch across the road is placed to alert everyone that a vehicle has broken down. It was too late to stop. The combination of the Harmadin winds, the car's weak head lights and the lack of warning lights caused Richard to skid about thirty meters before he hit the army truck. However, when the police witnessed the accident, he ran up to the car and tried to open the driver's door and couldn't because it was too damaged. Then the policeman was able to take Michael out of the passenger's side. Just that morning, before Richard and Michael departed, I asked Michael to put on his seat belt, but he chose not to since it isn't mandatory in Burkina Faso. Suddenly, the car caught on fire, and the policeman backed away, quite sure that the car would blow up. At that moment, the policeman noticed two tall Burkinabé women carrying large ceramic pots of water on their heads. They poured the water on the fire and put it out. Again the policeman attempted to free Richard from the car, and after an hour he finally got his door open. Then the policeman heard Richard speak these words, "I am sorry Michael that I can't save you, I tried so hard, but I couldn't save you." At that point Richard became unconscious. The policeman then called an ambulance to take them to the General African Hospital around 8:30 p.m.

Later on when the policeman tried to find these two women to thank them, no one knew who they were. They were not to be found in any villages near by. And no one would carry water on their heads at night because there are no street lights. Our final conclusion to the mysterious women was that they must have been angels.

When I finally found Richard lying on his small cot, all I could do was scream and scream. I could hardly recognize him. His face was twice its size with pieces of glass and small cuts all over. There were crusts of blood splattered on his face, arms and hands. His left wrist was broken and hanging by the skin. His forehead was dented in and I wondered if he would ever be normal again. At that moment, Rachelle and Richard both reassured me that everything would be fine, and that he would survive.

When the Canadian Ambassador and the ADRA Director of Burkina Faso arrived, they told us that they had called the ambulance to take Richard from this African General Hospital since there was no medical care. They wanted to transfer him to a French Clinic for the time being. They asked me to what country I wanted Richard flown, because they felt he should not be treated in Africa. My mind was in a fog and I couldn't think straight. I asked Richard if he wanted to be flown to Europe, United States or Canada? His response surprised us all. He said with confidence that he wanted to be treated here at the French Clinic. He wasn't planning on going home, for he believed he should identify with the Africans who suffered each day from very serious illnesses and sometimes death. Down deep in my heart, I truly wanted to go home, but knew that Richard had made up his mind, so I supported his decision.

Before Richard left the African hospital, he saw Michael on the floor, and asked the doctor to put him on a stretcher too, and bring him along, but the doctor said that Michael had to stay because he had no medical coverage. However, Richard wouldn't give up asking the doctor and told him that he would write Christians in Canada and appeal to them to send money to afford medical care for Michael. Finally, the doctor gave the okay to bring Michael with them.

Before going to the clinic, the ambulance made a stop at an x-ray laboratory, a separate building. It was now around 4a.m., and Rachelle and I were sitting in the foyer awaiting the verdict as to how serious the patients' injuries were. If anyone would have asked me what stood out in my mind during this entire ordeal, I would have answered that when I sat in that x-ray building and the loud Muslim chanting was heard over the PA speakers to call their people to worship, all I could think of was, "Why are the Muslims calling their people to worship now? Don't they care that my husband was in a serious car accident and might not live?"

After the x-rays were taken, Michael and Richard were placed once again in an ambulance that looked like a 1950 model. Once at the French Clinic, the African doctor told Richard that they had to operate on Michael first, since his liver was cut in several pieces and he had internal bleeding. The doctor also said that he doubted if Michael would make it and gave him about two hours to live. Of course, that was devastating news for us and Richard withdrew within himself. When they operated on Michael, the doctor could only use clean cloths to try to stop some of the bleeding, then sew him up to wait for death to take him. Next Richard was taken to the operating room to have his wrist worked on. All we could do was pray and wait for God's healing.

The doctor should have called for a bone specialist to see Richard's wrist because he could only put it in a sling and bring him back to bed. There the doctor began plucking several pieces of glass from Richard's face, arms and hands. It was very painful, but Richard tried not to squirm. A few days later, Michael was still breathing and speaking in a very low voice. But he was delirious most of the time. Needless to say, we weren't getting much sleep and food was not appealing. Each day and evening, several people from our church came to visit both patients and prayed constantly for a miracle healing. On the fourth day, Michael's fever returned to normal, and he asked for some soup. The doctor was so shocked that he was still alive. Now it was evident that he was going to live. The doctor told Richard he'd never seen a miracle from God before. The doctor was Catholic however, he asked Richard if he would give him Bible studies, knowing that he was a minister. That made two miracles in a row.

There was concern about Richard's eyes because of glass in them, and also about his dented forehead. Since the clinic wasn't equipped with technology, the doctor recommended that Richard be flown to the Ivory Coast where a specialist would give him a head scan and have his eyes checked. Our ADRA Director was a pilot and flew a small plane. He volunteered to fly Richard and me to the Abidjan Airport in Ivory Coast, to see these specialists in one of the hospitals. I made last minute arrangements with Rachelle and Andrea to be taken care of by the ADRA Director's wife, Georgette, while we were gone. We didn't know how long it would take before we returned, but we felt better that someone was looking after them.

While in the small plane flying among clouds, I felt I could almost touch them; they seemed so close. I began wishing that Jesus would come right at that moment and take us the rest of the way to our heavenly mansion. I didn't see the purpose for prolonging His return. I realized that it was only a selfish wish.

When we landed at the Abidjan Airport there was an ambulance waiting for us. Our pilot said good-bye to us and left right away and the ambulance drove us away from the airport towards an unknown hospital. There was a worker from our Division office who escorted us to the hospital and made sure that all the paperwork for Richard's medical bill was in order. Then we waited for a long time, wondering when we would see the specialist. Finally, the disappointing news came that we'd been brought to the wrong hospital by mistake. I decided we might as well make the best of it and asked at the nurse's station if they had a head scanner machine that could test for head injuries? They did, so an appointment was made for Richard, and a few hours later he was taken to another room to have his scan. The good news came that his head was fine with no internal injuries.

By then it was getting late in the evening and I had to find a place to stay. There were no extra beds for families at the hospital. So the Division man who'd stayed with me, offered to get me a ride to an Adventist Hostel where they rented small rooms. I was grateful for at least a bed.

The next day I got a ride to the Division office. Upon entering the office, I was surprised that most people had heard about Richard's car accident. I joined the group for their morning devotion. When it came to prayer requests Richard's name came up and they prayed for him, among other people. I didn't know what my next step would be, except that I needed a ride to the hospital. When I was contemplating whom to ask for a ride, I overheard a gentleman speaking English. Since only French and other African languages were spoken here, I looked toward the door where the English person was standing. He approached me and asked if I was Richard Parent's wife, and when I nodded in the affirmative, he then invited me into his office.

Once inside, Milton McHenry, an American missionary, told me that he and his wife Carol just arrived from the United States. He was the new Division ADRA Director centered in Ivory Coast, and Carol wasn't working as yet. He said Carol would be glad to see someone from her own culture and especially someone who spoke English. She soon arrived, and as we were talking she asked questions about the car accident, and what hospital Richard was in. Then she said, "Did you know that the hospital Richard's in is not a good one anymore. It used to have a very good reputation when Canadian Health Caretakers ran it. In fact, it was the best hospital in Abidjan at one time, but it has slowly deteriorated from neglect when the Canadian managers and staff left." She added that, "Some people in that hospital became worse, and some died who had not been that sick when they arrived." That bit of news did worry me.

Carol was still learning how to get around the chaotic city, but she volunteered to drive me to see Richard at the hospital. After introductions, she explained to Richard about the dangers of staying in that hospital, so he decided to sign himself out. We were invited to stay as long as we needed at the Mc Henry's home in Abidjan, Ivory Coast. What a restful and comfortable time we had there for the week we stayed.

Back home again, just when I thought our lives were about to settle into some kind of normal routine, Richard had another doctor's appointment and was told that his left wrist hadn't healed properly and he was scheduled for another surgery the day after we took Rachelle and my niece, Andrea to the Ouagadougou airport. They were flying back to school in Kenya after the Christmas break. With a sad look on our faces and loads of hugs we said good-bye, promising to see them for their June 2002, graduation at Maxwell Academy. From the airport we'd gone straight to the hospital for Richard would have his second operation on his wrist. Unfortunately, there were no hospital beds available in the general ward so Richard ended up on the maternity ward. We spent several hours with Richard, then the mission chauffeur drove me back home. That evening I received an e-mail from the Administrator from the Adventist Maxwell Academy in Kenya where Rachelle and Andrea were going to school. Mrs. Edwards mentioned that she and her husband had gone to the Nairobi airport to pick up Rachelle and Andrea who were coming from Burkina Faso, but they were not at the airport.

Around midnight the telephone rang. It was Rachelle, calling to say that the administrators at the Ghana airport wouldn't let her and Andrea on the plane. The custom at the Ghana airport is to over-book the planes and then decide who will board and who won't. The officials were looking for a bribe, but since Rachelle had no money to give them, she couldn't board the plane. It was an oversight on my part not to give her extra money. In the past things had been pretty straight forward--Rachelle would board the plane at Ghana, then fly to Ethiopia, and the last stop would be the Nairobi airport in Kenya without a hitch. This time she'd spent her last dollar to call me and had no more money. At least Rachelle was not alone in this dilemma. She and Andrea were able to support each other, and God was protecting them in Ghana.

I told her to contact ADRA personnel for help. Then the telephone went dead, and I was left with an awful empty feeling. Rachelle and Andrea were only seventeen, not old enough to be stranded in another country. I was grateful that at least Rachelle wasn't alone, but this call left me helpless. It became difficult to pray to God for help. I wasn't aware that I was in shock, and couldn't express my emotions, let alone spend time praying to the Lord. All I hoped for was a miracle_

I couldn't let Richard know about the girls dilemma yet. He was in the hospital, scheduled for surgery the next day. Being drained of strength and courage, I continually repeated in my mind the Bible text, "I can do all things through Christ which strengthens me." Phil.4:13 NIV. Around midnight, I called the Canadian Ambassador, a French Canadian, living in Ouagadougou. Judging by his hoarse voice, I got him out of bed. Instantly I apologized and told him my problem. He said that he would do everything in his power in the morning, when the Kenyan embassy opened.

It was encouraging to hear his next words, "I recall meeting your daughter Rachelle at the hospital," he said. "She struck me as having a lot of inner strength and courage. I know she will survive this ordeal." His words comforted me at the time, just when I needed it the most. I felt more alone and forsaken than ever before, since we only arrived six weeks ago in Africa. Afterwards, I realized that I passed through my Garden of Gethsemane experience.

Needless to say, I didn't sleep much that night, and I awoke early thinking constantly about the girls safety and how Richard was doing. I planned to visit him at the hospital after I did some office work that needed attention. There were decisions to be made and letters to answer in Richard's absence. I'd been thrust into that role since Richard's accident. The office distraction kept me from worrying so much. The next morning when I was going to the office, I saw two white doves perched on the ground. They seemed to be looking up at me. This was an unusual sight, but I took it as a positive omen from the Lord. No sooner did I enter the office when the telephone rang. It was the associate ambassador who told me that as she spoke, the girls were walking into the Nairobi airport. The girls had to wait three days at the Ghana Airport before they could board the plane to Kenya. What a relief to hear this good news; it was music to my ears. I went around the office broadcasting the joyous news.

Later that morning, when I arrived to visit Richard, he was out in the hall speaking to the pregnant Muslim ladies. He said, "Well, I am waiting to deliver soon, too." I gently nudged him into his room. His behavior surprised me. However, I discovered he was still strongly medicated they'd given him during his surgery, and he was playing the comedian. At least I could laugh for a change. It helped to relieve some of my pent up emotions.

Life took on a whole new meaning with more responsibilities.Some of the African Division and Union Conference leaders flew to our city and arranged to be guest speakers at our church in Ouagadougou, Burkina Faso. It meant that they planned to stay at our house upon their arrival for a weekend or a week. These guests were people I'd never met before. In normal circumstances, that didn't propose a problem, however, the timing hadn't been the best with Richard in the hospital, and Rachelle gone missing. I don't know what I would have done without our full-time cook and housekeeper.

That afternoon I received an e-mail from Mrs. Edwards, the administrator of Maxwell Academy saying how relieved she'd been to see the girls at the airport. However, they were seriously ill and had to be hospitalized. Apparently they drank some contaminated water at Ghana airport, and contacted a serious influenza. They'd also lost all their luggage and had no change of clothes during their delay. It took three weeks for the girls to recuperate before returning to school. Three weeks after the accident occurred I'd contacted the General Conference Headquarters of our church in Maryland, to tell them about what happened to Richard. Also, I mentioned about Rachelle's missing suitcases and inquired if there was any insurance coverage for this. The answer was no, but a few days later I received a letter from the GC saying that the entire staff had taken up a collection of $1,500. to help with the losses. I was touched to read about their generosity and I didn't know how to thank them enough. Of course, the most difficult call I had to make was to my family and Richard's. The families were so shocked and saddened, but they told me if there was anything they could do, to call. After that, Richard's family called regularly, wanting to hear his voice.

Richard was in the hospital almost three weeks. I'll never forget what happened next. I was sitting in church on Sabbath when I saw Richard walk into the church looking for me. He noticed the shocked look on my face when he sat down beside and gave me a contented smile in return. Obviously, he knew I was waiting for an explanation. He simply stated that he'd become bored sitting in the hospital bed all day and decided to sign himself out of the hospital. There was a gleam in his eye that said he made the right choice.

Even though the doctor told Richard not to return to work for three months, that didn't deter Richard to begin working four weeks after his accident. A month later he was doing a stop-smoking program. Through the advertisement in the local paper, the media came out, along with over three hundred people to attend the program. Richard did look awkward and funny with both arms in casts.

Life began to settle down, finally, and there were no immediate emergencies to tend to. I decided I wanted a tutor to teach me advanced French. So I contacted the Union Administrator about my request and they were glad to pay for lessons up to six months. I became busy taking classes with a very capable Burkinabé French tutor who met with me four days a week for six months. We became good friends and she often came to our home for social visits.

When I felt up to traveling, (if I wasn't stricken with malaria), I would travel with Richard to the various villages around Burkina Faso, visiting the members of newly built Adventist churches. There were always plenty of baptismal candidates ready for baptism. A year and a half after Richard's car accident, he'd baptized over five hundred people. It is amazing how the Lord brought triumph out of tragedy.

After a year of living in Burkina Faso, I was struck down four different times by malaria leaving me weak, delirious, and with no appetite. The strange thing about malaria is that it can attack any part of the body, and at first it doesn't seem like there are any definite symptoms. In my case, I had a toothache that persisted for two weeks and I tried to treat it with Tylenol daily. However, the left side of my face swelled up so badly that my eye closed. I went to a local dentist because our ADRA dentist was on vacation in Brazil. When I showed my left cheek to the local dentist she investigated my sore tooth and said that it needed to be pulled right away.

From experience, I knew that when the mouth and cheek are swollen, the dentist doesn't usually pull the tooth, but instead prescribes antibiotics. So I politely declined, and searched for a another dentist, who was originally from Germany. She told me that she wouldn't touch my tooth before I went to the French doctor at the clinic. The medical doctor took one look at me and asked what kind of medication I was allergic to? I told him I had allergic reactions from penicillin. He observed my cheek and asked what I was taking for my toothache, and I told him, Tylenol pain killers. He told me if one is allergic to penicillin, Tylenol will give the same reaction. Something I didn't know before. After two needles injected into my skin and a list of prescriptions, I went home thinking I'd soon feel much better. After a week the swelling in the cheek went down and my left eye reopened. But I still felt weak, delirious, and had no appetite.

Richard and I were taking prophylactics to prevent malaria, so thought we would never get it. Since prophylactics help prevent a person from high fevers or high temperatures, malaria was ruled out. Our co-workers in the office were concerned that I might have cholera since I'd been sick for six weeks. During office worship the staff prayed for me to get better. Then one day, Richard's treasurer suggested that we make an appointment with an African doctor that he knew who had a good reputation. So I went to see him. First he asked me my symptoms and I told him, then he told me he would give me a fifteen minute malaria test to determine if I had it or not. I thought this might be a waste of time.

Sure enough, the test revealed that I had malaria and that it was very serious. The doctor gave me prescriptions for different malaria pills, to which my body didn't respond so finally he recommended the strongest malaria medicine which finally healed that bout. However, it returned three more times. These silent microscopic mosquitoes that no one can see except under a microscope are active at night. But because of the extreme heat we hadn't protected ourselves in bed with netting.

About six months later, Richard had a bout of malaria that attacked his right ear. He said it was a huge drum-like thumping sound that wouldn't quit. After two weeks of this plus consistent ear pain, he was checked for malaria by the same doctor I'd seen. We discovered two things about malaria: prophylactics will not prevent everyone from contacting malaria, and African doctors are experts in discovering whether or not someone has it. After living in Burkina Faso, working in the mission office, and traveling weekends around the country to meet hundreds of Burkinabès, I developed a deep love and respect for these people. Even though I couldn't speak the thirty-four tribal languages of Burkina Faso, we communicated with them in the language of love that binds different cultures together.

I noticed how appreciative and grateful they were to the foreign missionaries. They know that without the on-going, large funding that comes from other countries to help build up their economy and improve their water supplies, they would be in crisis. So they truly are a nation that works very hard to gain foreigners' respect. They are a proud yes, gentle race, and we were glad to share in their culture and traditions. However, one thing that we were told by Africans was that they have no respect for foreigners who get angry and lose their tempers. It revealed a lack of self control, and the Burkinabés have plenty of self-control. They suffer in silence and rarely complain. They admire foreigners too, who have great respect for their culture, who are approachable, and who show genuine interest in their lives. Like all human beings, our needs are very similar.

Even though I wasn't a trained nurse, I played the part of one when some of the office staff and members of the church had motorbike accidents. I was fortunate to have a medical kit that Richard's sister, Nora, a nurse in Canada, had given me. It was stocked with all kinds of bandages, gauze, antiseptics, scissors and band-aids. It seemed that every two days I was running to the office or the church with my medical kit.

The largest Adventist Church in Burkina Faso is situated on the mission compound, where we lived, and the church is packed with families and children very early each Sabbath. The people are on fire for the Lord. We always sensed the spirit of God at work when members gave testimony after testimony of how God is active in their lives. On Sabbath, Mossi, the main African language is translated into French, and for the Ghanese, French is translated into English.

Each Sabbath the choir members wear their traditional red long gowns and caps, much like the traditional American graduation gowns with caps. They form a line outside of the church and file in one by one, singing a hymn as they walk softly to their seats in the front rows. It sets a spiritual atmosphere in the church, before the speaker gives a spiritual message from the platform.

Richard's mission office was situated beside the church, and he wanted to bond with as many people who entered the office as possible. One day Richard mounted on the wall a talking plastic fish who sang the song about, "don't worry be happy." When Richard invited people into his office to hear the singing fish their eyes would sparkle with joy as they laughed and felt very amused.

There are many adjustments and culture changes that missionaries must face in foreign countries, if they are to be effective in their churches and communities. What was heartbreaking to us was Adventist children and babies dying of SIDA (AIDS), and Meningitis. We remember a church family who had AIDS; the parents and their three children. We often invited them into our home for meals. Before we left Burkina Faso for good, these same friends gave us some beautiful homemade linen table cloths as a parting gift.

In the city of Ouagadougou, many merchants come from the villages daily to sell their products of fruits, vegetables, and wide selections of homemade traditional clothes and various items. The entrepreneurs spoke French as well as their tribal language. Richard and I were able to communicate with those who spoke French. Most of these vendors were women. They rise at 5a.m. each morning, feed their families, and then bring their children with them. The baby is tied around the mother's waist, and the other children ride on the motorbike that their mother drives. She balances a basket on her head that usually contains some sort of fruits or vegetables that she plans to sell that day. By 6 a.m. she is in her stall with all her products set up ready for business. Burkinabés do this kind of work seven days a week from early morning until late at night. The women are the real entrepreneurs in Burkina Faso, West Africa. Millions of proud women can be seen riding their motorbikes around the city of Ouagadougou. In the meantime, the men stay home and putter around doing odd jobs and riding their bicycles around the village, while the women carry heavy baskets or firewood on their heads.

As with music, art is also a part of the culture of Burkina Faso. The country hosts the International Arts and Crafts Fair which is one of the most important African handicraft fairs in the world.

Staring poverty in the flesh, daily, is truly a culture shock for any foreigner. Richard and I would walk to the market place often, and there crawling on the ground were bodies with no legs and feet. They were full of dirt as they dragged their upper bodies down the road. Of course, foreigners would be surrounded by adults and children begging for food and money. This behavior was difficult to watch. We knew that we couldn't give many coins to all the poor. Before we went to Africa, a returned missionary from there told us at our International Mission class in Michigan, that for the first year, missionaries who are exposed to extreme poverty, feel helpless, and depressed because they have no control over the dilemma. Then gradually they begin to realize they can have some input into relieving some of the suffering, but not all, and they can make a difference. Finally, life takes on a whole new meaning as they affect the lives of the devastated.

After two years of living in this unique country, we sensed, after much praying, that the Lord wanted us to move. It wasn't easy to make this decision because of our love and devotion to the African Burkinabés. We knew that if we stayed longer, malaria would weaken us to the point where we would develop serious health problems. Richard had almost completed his doctorate of theology by correspondence with the University of South Africa, and he'd learned a lot as an administrator and president of the Burkina Faso mission. However, he always desired to become a teacher of theology, helping students to become dedicated ministers.

He sent his resumé to different Christian Adventist Universities in Africa, including Madagascar, and he received a positive response from Pastor Paul Pichot, the Rector of the Adventist University of Zurcher, in Madagascar, inviting him to teach theology courses for the September, 2002 semester. Now a new chapter was being added to our missionary journey.

"It seems that every time you think you are ready to graduate from the school of experience, somebody thinks up a new course"
by Education Digest

CHAPTER 23

LIVING WHERE THE LEMURS LIVE

The island of Madagascar is in the Indian Ocean, off the southeastern coast of Africa, and is the fourth largest island in the world, comparable in size to Kenya. The cartoon "Madagascar" is nothing like the real island. The only wild animals that exist there are lemurs and crocodiles.

The population of this island is a mix of Asians and Africans. There are some Arabs, and East Indians. The main language is of Malayo-Polynesian origin and is uniquely spoken throughout the island. French is spoken mainly among the educated population of this former French colony. English, although rare, is being taught in the primary grades of forty-four schools with Peace Corps volunteers training teachers. The government began this pilot project in 2003.

The main religions in Madagascar are Roman Catholic, Reformed Protestant, Lutheran and Anglican. About 45% of the Malagasy are Christians, Divided almost evenly between Roman Catholics and Protestants.

We first arrived at the Antananarivo Airport, Madagascar, from West Africa, on September 27, 2002, two weeks before school was to begin. Usually the University of Zurcher starts school every September, but due to the civil war that had taken place in Madagascar, with bridges being blown up, lack of petro, and rationing of food and water, the country was paralyzed. Richard and I arrived in Madagascar right after the civil war ended. The wooden bridges were rebuilt, but the country's economy had plummeted and the nation was in peril.

Since Richard was teaching several theology courses each semester, he had a lot of syllabi to type from scratch. There are no textbooks available for students to study from, mainly because of lack of funds. Each teacher in theology, business, and computer science must make up their own textbooks for the subjects they teach. With only two weeks left to work a miracle, Richard stayed up very late each night well into the semester, attempting to stay ahead of his curriculum.

The new President Ravalomanana of Madagascar was elected in September, 2002 was already beginning to make good changes in his country. Since we just arrived around the same time, what we clearly remember were employer's wives and myself from the university would do our marketing each week in Antsirabe, a town that was a half hour from University of Zurcher where we lived. The smell of sewage and dirt would be hard to forget when walking down the broken up streets. However, after about a year of shopping in town, President Ravalomanana had constructors build new sewages and paved roads. The dirt and smell finally disappeared from Antsirabe and shopping became much more bearable.

At our school we became good friends with one of the students, John Ravelomanantsoa, who grew up with President Ravalomanana. They went to school and played together as youngsters. Since we found it difficult to pronounce the students long names such as those mentioned above, we opted to call the Malagasies by their first names. It saved a lot of embarrassment and time.

Madagascar is isolated from the rest of the continents. It has a unique mix of plants and animals, many found nowhere else in the world. The eastern side of the island is considered tropical rainforest while the southern sides are home to tropical dry forests.

A system called "slash-and-burn" **(tavy)** has reduced forest trees, and applied pressure to endangered species. This method of "slash and burn"is used by shifting cultivators to create short term yields from soils. Since it is practiced often in these forest areas, without intervening fallow periods, the nutrient-poor soils are eroded to an unproductive state. These frequent tavy procedures have caused increased sedimentation to western rivers.

More than once Richard and I with several students and faculty members, had to try to put out huge forest fires around our university with branch switches, because there were no firemen or fire trucks that exists in Madagascar. Local farmers would start the fires to create clouds in the air, hoping to bring rain. Small trickles of rain would fall from the clouds, but never enough to drench the ground. This practice exists all over Madagascar and has caused much damage, not only to the soil, but to surrounding homes.

Agriculture, along with and forestry, is a mainstay of the economy. Major exports are coffee, vanilla, sugarcane, cloves, cocoa, rice, cassava (tapioca), beans, bananas, peanuts and livestock products.

The northern and eastern coast regions have fairly hot temperatures since they are situated near the Indian Ocean. However, the climate is different in the central region of Madagascar where we lived in the mountain region. We found the weather to be moderate, not too extreme hot or cold. There seem to be two seasons. Summer begins around November until May, and winter begins in June until November. Temperatures during the summer go up to 75 degrees Fahrenheit during the day, down to 50 degrees at night. However, the winter temperature can dip down in the 30 degree range, and a few times we experienced temperatures as low as minus 6. Winter can be very uncomfortable without proper heating in the homes, even though there are primitive fireplaces, the firewood is expensive. So we wore our winter coats and boots in the homes most of the time. Classrooms also were not heated and students have to endure harsh winters.

In the central region, where we lived, forestry consisted of mainly eucalyptus trees, and tall thin pines. Multitudes of huge colorful poisonous spiders like to make their webs in these trees.

Recently in the news, in early May, 2008, a horrific cyclone swept over Myanmar (Burma) and killed over 22,000 people--a devastating blow. It brings to mind the cyclonic storms that struck Madagascar when we were living at our University Adventist Zurcher in January, 2005. There are several strong electrical storms in the central region that can persist for several months. In February and March of that year, there were six cyclones that struck our campus furiously and leveled hundreds of campus trees, mainly pine. Unfortunately, the trees in that area are not deeply rooted in the poorly uncultivated soil and cannot withstand severe storms. The eastern and northern coasts felt the cyclones even more with hundreds of casualties, not to mention crop failures, and loss of cattle. When the cyclones struck our area, we were fortunate the cyclone hit high above our homes, otherwise there could have been more destruction and possible deaths.

Since Madagascar is south of the equator, cyclones are prevalent. They are similar to hurricanes except cyclones twirl in the opposite direction. In fact, even toilets there flush in the opposite direction to toilets in other countries.

It wasn't unusual to spend many nights without electricity, with candles as our only source of light to cook and study by. The lack of electricity played havoc with the food in the refrigerator and the frozen produce in an old freezer we had shipped to Madagascar. I remember spending many nights praying that our food would not be spoiled. When I wasn't praying about that, there was the lack of water to pray about. At times, our water pump, which operated our well system on campus broke. There was another water well for reserve only, so we would be on water rations. For about three months everybody jumped out of bed around 5:30 a.m. to take a shower and quickly filled the three large pails with water to last until the next morning.

I recall one graduation weekend at the university, in early June, 2005, when all the faculty families had to invite the guest speakers who came from the South Indian Ocean Division in Africa, to their different homes for a meal. I signed up to have the ministerial secretary of SID, South Indian Division, and his family for a Friday night meal. While preparing the meal all I could think about was having enough water to boil the pasta I was planning to cook for their supper. The main water line was shut off to preserve water for the graduation weekend. I prayed and prayed until I heard a knock at the door. Our friendly maintenance man, Diyan Dinev, was standing at the door. He had gladly announced that the water would be turned on for an hour so that everyone could fill up their pails for the weekend. It was a relief to know that I'd had enough water to cook plus wash the dishes after dinner.

It didn't take long to discover that the only hydro plant in Madagascar was in a crisis. Around 2004, the only electrical company in Madagascar was going bankrupt. The hydro was going to be cut off, because it owed millions of dollars, due to fraud. The president quickly resolved the problem by appealing to the Quebec Hydro of Canada for help and received it.

Unfortunately, in Madagascar, some times fraud is very prevalent where business is concerned. One incident comes to my mind when my husband and I arranged with ADRA in British Columbia, Canada, to have a huge container shipped to Madagascar containing all kinds of basic items for the Malagasy people. However, unknown to us, the Malagasy man we thought could be trusted, and who acted as a middle man at the custom's office on the school's behalf, stole most of the ADRA container goods, and left the school only a few items.

When we returned permanently home to North America, we received some good news and bad news from our friend, Milton Zamora, a computer science teacher at our university in Madagascar, on January 22, 2008 . The good news was that renovation and rearrangement of the UAZ library was completed, in addition to three building constructions of the new classrooms and department offices, and the completion of the police outpost beside the school. However, the bad news is that on January 22, 2008, the supervisor of maintenance and construction manager, Roger Pelayo, and his eight workers were working on extending the cafeteria. Suddenly a strong electrical storm was brewing, when the crew decided to take a small break and sat on a pile of wood. On sudden impulse Roger Pelayo left the group for a few minutes to do something, and as a result saved his life. The rain was teaming down, and a loud crash of lightening struck the group and they fell to the ground harming six and killing two workers. Despite the losses and destruction caused by the electrical storm, this devastating experience drew the campus closer together as they tried to comfort the families and friends in the blessed hope of Jesus' soon return.

Many Malagasies incorporate the cult of the dead in their religious beliefs, and bless their dead at church before proceeding with the traditional burial rites. They also may invite a pastor to attend a "famadihana," or "turning over the dead." Each family is responsible to perform this costly ritual every five years in honor of their dead. From June until September practice of the "famadihana" (turning over the dead) takes place each year. Richard and I attended such a celebration.

Richard and I, and some of our school staff witnessed over twenty bodies, new and old, being taken from their Mausoleum while the family members peeled off the old cloths from the dead bodies, replacing them with new expensive linen cloths. Many poor families go into debt to celebrate this ritual. If some members of the family, do not want to partake of the "famadihana", the cult of the dead, due to different religious beliefs, than the family members are disowned by their families and their plot of land is taken from them.

Another Malagasy cultural practice that is presently changing is the "trial marriages" that parents fully encourage. The interested couple are to live together for a year in order to produce a baby, and if that doesn't happen the parents insist that the couple separate and try another partner until the girl is pregnant then and only then do the parents give permission to marry. However, this tradition is changing, and more and more parents now allow their young adults to choose their own marriage partner and wed rather than try "trial marriages."

When buying honey in Madagascar it is necessary to ask where the honey came from first. Apparently, in some areas of Madagascar some dead bodies are put in wooden coffins and placed high up in trees. At times bee hives decide to make their homes in the coffin. What happens next is bee hive growers take the honey produced by the bees in the coffins and sell it in jars to the public. There apparently are no legal health rules regarding produce of any kind.

Music to the Malagasies is as natural as breathing They play different home-made instruments with a lot of vigor and energy. It is a real treat to see them perform. They also enjoy being in center stage, whether it is playing instruments, singing, dancing or acting or worshiping. They just love performing in whatever capacity they can. The Malagasies begin singing at a very young age, around three or four years old, in public. Perhaps that is why they experience no stage fright when they perform in front of huge audiences. Their voices sound so melodious and soft, that they raise goose pumps on my arms whenever they are singing. They play by ear, and most of them have never had a music lesson in their lives. Even if some of them wanted to take lessons, they could never afford them. Even so, music is their first love and they can play or sing for hours without feeling tired. When we get to heaven, I won't be surprised if the Malagasies are our choir leaders and music teachers.

I recall that it was right after our passports had to be renewed in 2003, I received word from home in Canada, that my mother had a stroke, and she was in a semi-conscious state. The doctor advised my siblings to come to the hospital since this could be the last time.

Unfortunately, our passports were at the Canadian Embassy in Africa instead of Madagascar because there were no Canadian Embassy. We frantically tried to trace down our passports since it was a good six months since we dropped off our old passports at the Canadian Consulate in Madagascar, and we needed our new ones right away just in case my mother turned for the worse.

In the meantime, my sisters sent us this funny letter regarding Mom's condition. She apparently woke up and noticed all her children around her hospital bed except me. When my siblings asked Mother how she was feeling, she had this puzzled look on her face and said , "Well, I am either going to die or get married," then went back to sleep.

Mom was a widow for several years and of course we knew that Mom was seeing a new Christian man who wanted to marry her, but we didn't realize that she was considering marriage, because she never brought it up before.

The story ended on a happy note because Mom ended up marrying this fine Christian gentleman and they spent several good years together until he passed away peacefully. Mom lived on a good many years herself until she passed away this February, 2010. Our family all have fond memories of our Mom whom we all miss.

We spent four weeks each summer beginning in July in Canada, which was Madagascar's winter. Of course, when it would be time to return to Madagascar for another school year we would pack all kinds of items in our suitcases, including funny gadgets that Richard would present in his classes. From time to time he would surprise the students by putting on these plastic eye glasses and buck teeth. He'd explained to them that he needs to find a dentist and an eye doctor because he can't see very well, and his teeth are falling out. At first the students would look at Richard very seriously, no laughter would be heard, until they noticed Richard was laughing. In time, the students would tell Richard some funny jokes and felt a rapport with their teacher.

The funniest incident that I recall happened one morning when I was getting ready for school and running late. I was looking for my beige pants in my closet but couldn't find them. Anyway, I wore another pair and ran to class. Out of breath, I sat down in my seat. Gradually I noticed that the pair of pants my husband was wearing were mine. We both lost a lot of weight, but I never thought he'd be able to fit into my pants. I leaned over to one of my student friends and said in French that my husband was wearing my pants by mistake. It didn't take long for the news to spread around the class and ripples of laughters drowned out Richard's voice. He suddenly stopped talking and asked the class, What was so funny." One of the students said that he was wearing his wife's pants. As he looked down at them Richard had to admit he was.

Instead of searching on campus for a full-time job, I decided to become a full time student of theology. Even though all of the courses were in French, I was determined to stick to my goal and complete a bachelor of theology degree in four years. It was the hardest job I've ever undertaken, and I was discouraged and worn out most of the time. However, my husband Richard was a strong inspiration, along with some friends on campus who kept praying for me. On May 21, 2006, several students graduated together, and we all felt so relieved to finally complete four years of a grueling task.

Foreign administrators wore many hats, having to perform different roles, including my husband who was a full time theology teacher, dean of theology, translator and year-book editor. He took all the photos of the students, faculty and the entire staff of the school, including kitchen staff, gardeners and security guards. Also, he was a translator at midweek prayer meetings, Friday night vespers, Sabbath church, and Sabbath afternoon programs and board meetings. He also gave sermons and seminars in the church once a month.

Every two months our rector's wife, Rupelin Pichot, the cafeteria manager, worked extra hard with some students to put together an entertaining Saturday night social. Many students came and participated in these important events. My husband,

Richard, was also asked to display funny photos by adding distorted images to everyone's pictures he'd taken on campus. Of course, everybody laughed when they saw their own familiar faces.

How can I describe the Malagasy people? In the four years that I lived in Madagascar at the University of Zurcher, we spent almost everyday with the students and staff. Also, twice a year, the faculty, staff and students took a few excursions together to the faraway north and east coasts of Madagascar. It has been my observation that the Malagasy are a peaceful and a gentle spirited people. They can be soft-spoken and very polite to foreigners. Several Malagasy are indirect when communicating with foreigners, whereas most foreigners are direct in their manner of speech. Living in Madagascar we learned being transparent and open in communication isn't a major issue for them. What really counts in this particular culture is that they keep face. Their pride is everything that they stand for as a race, as opposed to being open and up front like in our North American culture.

Deep friendships among the Malagasy are possible, but with a lot of effort, patience, and earned trust on the foreigners' part. Of course, it is true that foreigners who don't know how to speak their language tend to feel more isolated and cut off. We discovered that even though the national language, French, is spoken by both foreigners and educated Malagasies, language barriers still existed. However, when we learned what their priorities in communication were, we began to understand and appreciate more of their diverse culture.

Cheating in the classes at the school was very common and teachers had quite a challenge dealing justly with it. When a student was caught cheating on an exam or test, their mark would be "0_. Eventually, as time went on, cheating declined.

One Sabbath Richard and I decided to take a long walk through the fields and the different trails that led around the school campus. At one point we noticed a huge, black, ferocious bull not far from us. In the past, the bulls we had noticed were bony with ribs protruding from their body and a docile look on their faces. However, this one was different. We walked a little farther down the trail toward him when suddenly we realized he was about to charge at us. Since we couldn't run away from him we jumped over the bushes and hid. Then a few seconds later we looked over the bushes to see where that black bull had gone. He wasn't where we thought he would be...Then we heard a noise behind us, and turned around to face this ferocious animal staring at us. As he charged at us, we quickly jumped over the bushes once again and ran as fast as our legs could go toward our house. Who would have known that we would have been chased by a ferocious black bull on a peaceful sunny Sabbath day?

A few weeks before the end of our last year at University Adventist Zurcher, we were completely surprised by three going away parties on our behalf. Knowing full well how poor and needy these students and staff were, we couldn't get over their gifts of love and generosity. There are valuable souvenirs of Madagascar that hang on our walls today as mementos.

We shall never forget one first year student who played the viola. This instrument sounds like a harp when played properly and only Anselme knew how. He displayed such confidence and played with ease. I get a little emotional when talking about him. The night of our going away party he presented us with a 'viola' similar to the one he played. He and his father had been Christian Adventists for three years. His father owned a small business which was doing well, so he was able to provide financially for his family. Since Anselme told him that Richard was leaving for good, his father had a viola made and presented it to us as a gift of love. Then a week later Anselme wasn't at school. When we enquired about his absence, the news was shocking and beyond belief. One of his father's workers had stolen a lot of money from Anselme's father then killed him, cut him up in small pieces, and left him in a ditch near his home. The entire school body grieved for Anselme and his family. In Madagascar when some tragedy happens to the father of a household, the remaining family suffer not only from grief but extreme poverty.

At last graduation came on May 21, 2006. There were a total of twenty graduates, including theology and business students. We had a full program that weekend. A week before we finished school, we had to decorate the large church. Since Richard and I visited our family in Canada each summer, we were able to bring back decorations for the graduation. We also had to find someone to build steps leading to the platform in the church since there were none. For previous graduation in 2005, there were no steps leading to the church platform so the students borrowed some cafeteria long tables to put against the platform and added a few steps leading to the tables so that the graduates, faculty and visiting senators could step on top of them in order to walk unto the platform. Richard and I didn't want to see that experience repeated again due to the risk involved. After praying diligently about who could build the steps, by March, we our maintenance man, Roger Pelayo, found some builders in town who accomplished the task in a short time.

We also had to practice several songs, in three different languages, for the weekend programs, along with short speeches. Sunday was the official graduation event. Several senators of Madagascar were invited to attend the ceremony along with guest speakers. It was a full program, and well organized graduation weekend. We were fatigued, but content that we'd accomplished a milestone in our lives, thanks to Jesus.

As students we shared a lot in those past four years. There were financial challenges for the Malagasy students, (hunger was their constant enemy), along with ill health and deprived sleep. Now that was over for them, at least for the time being. We had to say good-bye to every graduate. It was very sad and a difficult time for all of us, knowing we'd never see them again.

For six summers, from 2000 to 2006, Richard and I had flown home to our families for vacations on furlough. In the summer of 2002 to 2006, we decided to fund raise for the elementary school and university in Madagascar. When we arrived in 2002, there were only six children attending elementary school. These students were the staff's children. So, when we returned home each summer on vacations, we packed our African and Malagasy costumes, and visited churches that wanted to hear about our experiences. One summer we were so delighted when we made appeals for student funding to receive a total of $7,000. When we returned to Madagascar, close to seventy-five elementary students enrolled from all the different villages around the school.

The university students also had also received helped with their tuition with these foreign funds we raised each summer, along with food staples such as rice, flour and pasta. One portion of the funds came from . A portion of the money came from a very generous teacher and one of our church members, Pamela Wilson, from our Barstow Church where my husband is presently the pastor.

Also, during the past three years, the Vacation Bible School leader, Mrs. Leyanne Roschman, also teacher and pastor's wife at Heritage Green Seventh-day Adventist Church in Hamilton, Ontario, Canada, organized a fund-raising program with the Vacation Bible School children in the church and community by going door to door, appealing for funds for the Malagasy elementary children in Madagascar. Some of the children saved their allowances for a long time each year. They raised funds each summer for the next three years. We can't help but marvel at the dedicated children and adults who sacrificially gave to our Malagasy students in great need from Canada.

We were thinking that when Richard and I left Madagascar permanently in May, 2006, for Canada, there might not be any more funding. But God came through and found another enthusiastic, and devoted donor at Heritage Nursing Home. Mrs. Carol Minnick, Activities Director. Her with her friends sell apples from someones orchards each Auturmn, and raise funds to continue the work that we started.

North Americans have always been extremely generous givers to third world countries, despite the sacrifices they make. God's timing never fails, as we were witnesses to God's unlimited supplies of blessings that spread graciously from others to these precious poor people.

Who would have thought that Richard and I would be part of God's vision to increase the small school population from five primary students to over two hundred at the present time. When we arrived at University of Zurcher in Madagascar in the year 2002 there was a small school classroom of five children who belonged to the school staff. Then God planted this seed in our hearts to expand the small classroom and open it up to under priviledged illiterate village children, including several children from the orphanage that was built on the school property. And how did God direct us? By fundraising in our churches back in Canada, and later to the United States each summer on furlough. Nearly 120 elementary students were sponsored, along with 18 college students.

Due to other sponsorships in the United States, Canada and Europe, and funds from the Division Headquarters, there are now several more school buildings built besides the expansion of the elementary school, and a new high school. Some other buildings include a new nursing classroom, and new girl's and boy's dormitories. Now every student can spend their entire years from elementary through to University to complete their bachelor degree in a Christian environment.

Without the dedicated and hard working missionaries like Roger and Evelyn Pelayo, along with Forsythia and Gabby Galgao, Milton and Daisie Zamora, not to mention Pastor Paul Pichot, the Recteur, and his wife Rupelin, there would not have been an opportunity for so many Malagasies to broaden their fields and fulfill their dreams, all the while perfecting their English and French. Praise God for His visionary resources that made the dreams of every staff member and student come true.

As a missionary you never run out of stories to tell. My last one is from a third- year student called Jahaziela Ramanitra, nineteen years old, and a friend of mine. He was very determined to learn English. Every time we met in class he would ask me to speak to him in English, and so I would. Halfway through his third year, he didn't come back to school, and again everybody was concerned about him missing so much. Of course, we tried to find out what happened, but it was many months later before he finally returned. Two weeks before graudation , May, 2006, he came to our home to explain why he'd been absent. With his head down, tears in his eyes, he quickly said, "I am sorry that I couldn't notify the school about my absence, but I was so sad and depressed about my dilemma that I didn't know where to start. About three months ago my father was murdered, and my mother disappeared, leaving me with three small siblings to care for. I was so worried about my mother's disappearance that I couldn't sleep at night. Finally, my mother came home unharmed, and I returned to school."

Our hearts and prayers reached out to him. We knew how difficult it was for him to talk about such a tragedy since he is a very quiet and private fellow.

"Every bird likes its own nest best" __ Proverb (French)

CHAPTER 24
PERMANENT RETURN

When Richard and I finally returned home to Canada for good in May 2006, we were jobless. Our only child and daughter, Rachelle, whose husband, Jeffrey, was in the Navy and stationed in San Diego, California. They called us to come for a visit shortly after we arrived home . However, a few church conferences from Chicago and Florida, called Richard and wanted to interview him for a possible position as a pastor, and since we already booked our flights to San Diego to vist our daughter, we postponed the interviews for awhile.

After spending some quality time, Richard received a call from the Southeastern Conference office, calling him to serve as a minister to the Barstow church, in Barstow, California. Even if we'd tried to work out our own plans to live close to our daughter and son-in-law, it wouldn't have worked out. It was clear to us that the Lord opened up the door of opportunity to serve in a location not far from where our daughter, and son-in-law lives.

About a year into our church ministry, one of our head elders, who was also a Lieutenant Colonel employed at the military base in Barstow, casually mentioned to Richard that the Barstow Community College was searching for a theology teacher with the right credentials to teach a few theology courses during the week. Since Richard didn't have his green card yet to allow him to work legally in the United States, he had to wait. Several months later when he did receive his green card it slipped his mind to apply as a theology teacher. Then one morning as I was having my private devotions the Lord laid this heavy burden on my heart that Richard should act and bring his school documents and degrees to Barstow College. Without an appointment we both arrived at the Administrators office looking for an interview with a Dr. Meadows. After Richard's impromtu interview, he was hired within a few days as a theology teacher. The amazing thing is that a week after Richard was hired Dr. Meadow transferred to San Diego University. God's timing is always on perfect timing. What a wonderful way to meet and minister to young people.

Not long after moving to California, a former Madagasy student by the name of Jahaziela, who told us his sad story about his father's murder, and his mother who ran away leaving Jahaziela with three small siblings, wrote Richard this heartfelt letter. We were surprised to receive a letter from this particular student, because he'd hardly ever expressed himself in class or even in social gatherings. At this time I would like to share his message with you.

He says, "Dear Mrs. & Mr. Parent, It's with a big honor that you were both with me at AUZ College in Madagascar. I think that we will meet in heaven, soon and very soon. You have made me rich by giving me the gift of hope, by teaching me how to live and to be a good theologian, by being there when I needed a friend, by being the best teacher for me, and by giving me a shove in the right direction when I hesitated. Thanks for bringing happiness to a heart full of woe, and for all the wonderful things you do. I found a true friend, when I found you"

We continue to be a link between these two worlds by our letters of encouragement and sometimes finances. The bonds of people from both worlds are a treasure we can always carry with us to heaven.

In May, 2010, I was faced with a scary medical diagnosis of cancer in April of 2010, by my Ob-Gyn. When being examined by Dr. Adam's office, she was surprised how the cancer was discovered since there were no pre-warning signs. Recently, I received a clear bill of health, and feel so much better. We praise the Lord for his healing hand, and bountiful grace.

Part of our summers is usually spent in Ontario, Canada with family and friends. However, this summer was different due to the fact that we siblings planned to take a long journey way up north, several hours away from Toronto. There we would return to our birth place of several years ago to bury Mom's ashes, and hold a small memorial.

When we arrived at our first hotel in Haileybury, an hour from Matachewan, Sandra announced to all us siblings, "We have more ashes than we know what to do with." At first I thought she was going to say that we forgot Mom's ashes, but no we have more ashes. Of course, we all had this puzzled look on our faces, not to mention that we just completed a nine hour trip and arrived close to our destination, tired and hungry. Sandra reassured us that Mom's ashes were not forgotten. What then could it be? Reluctantly, she went to explain why we have extra ashes. She went on to explain, " my next door neighbour's son, Ron, had parents that died about 5 years ago and he wanted to put their ashes in a river or lake where his parents used to live in the north, a couple hours drive from where we were going to bury Mom's ashes. I mentioned to Ron that we were planning a trip soon to Matachewan, nine hours north of Toronto, and Ron must have taken this as a sign from God, because he promptly asked me an unusual favour, would I be willing to take his parents' ashes with us and find a small lake in Sudbury to bury the ashes?" That explains the extra ashes in the two urns, besides Mom's, in the van, unbeknown to some of the siblings. When we heard the reason for the extra ashes our puzzled looks quickly turned into sheer shock.

A few hours later, after we held Mom's memorial in Matachewan, we arrived in Sudbury, with no clue as to which body of water we should throw this couples' ashes. One of us spotted a smaller lake with no people around, called "Richard's Lake." How appropriate since that was my husband's name. As we got out of the van with the two urns in a large bag we immediately noticed a lady peering out of her living room window at us. We knew that it was somewhat illegal to throw people's ashes in any lake, but we were on a mission to help our sister, Sandra, with this unusual request. This spectator at her window made us a bit nervous, but we tried to act as nonchalant as possible as we continued walking down the path that led to our final destination.

Quickly Richard took the urns out of the bag, lifted the lids and noticed that the ashes were wrapped in plastic. He proceeded to surgically cut the bags with his pocket knife, and as he vigourously poured the ashes into the lake, a strong wind suddenly picked up and bits of the ashes landed in our faces and between our toes. Imagine what we sounded like as we as we sputtered out the words from Psalm 23.

After that ritual was finished we nervously went back to the van minus the urns. The same lady was still glued to her window, and we wondered if she had already called the police. Once back in the van we searched quickly for a dumpster to throw the urns in since the son didn't want them back. Jokingly Richard said that maybe we should open up a business, and call it, "Ashes Are Us."

My story ends where it began with three innocent siblings who died in my parent's house by fire many years ago in a small mining town of Matachewan. My sisters Sandra and Nadine purchased a beautiful large grey granite tombstone with two hearts carved on top with Mom and our siblings' names on it. The tombstone arrived not long before we did, and it was placed in the ground in the Matachewan Cemetery. There we held an memorial on behalf of Mom and her three children. The gentle rain that began to fall seemed appropriate as we had shed some tears of sadness and even joy because at last Mom's journey is over and she finally joins her three little children to await Jesus' return. What happiness there will be when Mom and her children are reunited in the resurrection, never to be apart from one other again.

My mother's challenge throughout her entire adult life was to accept her three children's untimely death, and her personal accountability.

We all live with some regrets, and that is why it is so important that we find true inner peace. In the Book of Romans 5:10, Paul reminds us, "For if, while we were enemies, we were reconciled to God through the death of His Son, then how much more, having been reconciled, will be saved by His life."

Though I made a number of detours in my life, the Lord rescued and protected me from many trials and danger. He continues to direct in all our lives who are willing to read Jesus' Love Letter to them, and to make things right in their lives, while they can.

Jeremiah 29:11, it reminds everyone that God's plans are not to harm us, but to make us prosper and have a promising future. These are words that I claim and carry in my heart daily.

If anyone who reads my life story will make a heart felt decision to follow Jesus, He will lead you. Only then will you have, not only a purposeful and happy life, but you will spend eternal life with Jesus, never to suffer death and separation again.

Through experiencing God throughout my life's journey, I discovered that God is real and personal. It is not a question of trying to make contact with some divine force that is inate in all of us, but to have a personal relationship with Jesus, our Saviour. Our Lord made this claim, "This is life eternal that they might know Thee, the only true God, and Jesus Christ whom Thou has sent."

CHAPTER 25

HELPFUL TIPS TO REACH NEW AGERS

Jesus characterized the time of His return this way:

"For many will come in My name, saying, 'I am the Christ,' and will deceive many." (Matthew 24:5 NKJV). "Then many false prophets will rise up and deceive many." (Matthew 24:11 NKJV). "For false christs and false prophets will rise and show great signs and wonders to deceive, if possible, even the elect." (Matthew 24:24 NKJV).

Would we be wise to assume that miracles are a proof that God is behind something?

"And I saw three unclean spirits like frogs coming out of the mouth of the dragon, out of the mouth of the beast, and out of the mouth of the false prophet. For they are spirits of demons, performing signs, which go out to the kings of the earth and of the whole world, to gather them to the battle of that great day of God Almighty." (Revelation 16:13-14 NKJV)

"The coming of the lawless one is according to the working of Satan, with all power, signs, and lying wonders" (2 Thessalonians 2:9 NKJV). "Now the Spirit expressly says that in latter times some will depart from the faith, giving heed to deceiving spirits and doctrines of demons" (1 Timothy 4:1 NKJV). "He performs great signs, so that he even makes fire come down from heaven on the earth in the sight of men. And he deceives those who dwell on the earth by those signs which he was granted to do in the sight of the beast, telling those who dwell on the earth to make an image to the beast who was wounded by the sword and lived." (Revelation 13:13-14 NKJV). "For such are false apostles, deceitful workers, transforming themselves into apostles of Christ. And no wonder! For Satan himself transforms himself into an angel of light. Therefore it is no great thing if his ministers also transform themselves into ministers of righteousness, whose end will be according to their works." (2 Corinthians 11:13-15 NKJV).

In today's society many assume that irrespective of what they get into there would be no repercussions. We are all involved in a spiritual warfare. In fact, just today, my daughter Rachelle called us to relate a troubling experience her and her husband Jeffrey had last evening. They were in bed sleeping when Rachelle described how she felt a heavy pressure and pains shooting to her chest and back. Suddenly there was a dark form floating by their bed. She immediately asked Jeffrey if he seen this dark form floating across their room, and Jeffrey said he had. They had this same experience about three years ago when they lived in San Diego.

Apparently Jeffrey shared with Rachelle that he's been having these apparitions since he was six years old, and that they leave him depressed and lacking energy. He feels there is no protection from these horrific evil spirits that would invade his sleep since he was a child.

Our prayers and our appeals to God will always be ascending to Heaven on their behalf. Friends these spiritual attacks are real and fearful. However, as Christians we need not fear

Satan and his evil spirits for we have the sure Word of God that He will never forsake us or leave us. We are to only call on the name of "Jesus Christ" and command Satan and his evil spirits to depart from us for they have no power over our Lord Jesus. When Satan hears an innocent frightened Christian call out Jesus name, Satan flees because he knows that he was a defeated foe at the cross, and that Christ is victorious over him.

Christians cannot be gullible as Satan is using sorcery, spirititism, angelology, the occult, and channeling which are all aspects of the modern New Age phenomonon. Some Christian ministers are encouraging their members to unlock their unconscious minds in order to have more power with God to get whatever they want. They think they can manipulate God so that He does what they want Him to do. "Therefore humble yourselves under the mighty hand of God, that He may exalt you in due time,." (1 Peter 5:6 NKJV). Modern thinking is urging us to preoccupy ourselves with "Self". But rather than self-love and self-esteem, and self-assertion, the Bible calls us to self-denial and self-control. Christ calls us to take up our crosses and follow Him. (Matthew 16:24, 25).

To build our lives on anything but Christ and His teachings is to build on sinking sand.

I have such a blessed assurance in Christ and His eternal plans for me, and I invite you to have the same. This certainty, and peace of mind I can find nowhere else.

CPSIA information can be obtained at www.ICGtesting.com
229675LV00003B/2/P

9 781936 780228